Mother is Coming
Home

ROGER EVANS

Table of Contents

Growing Up in McDowell County, West Virginia

THERE ARE MANY stories about growing up in McDowell County, West Virginia—some of hardship, some of joy—and how we were all changed forever by spending our childhood there. My story is about all of that: hardship, joy, and how it affected my adult life. Thanks to so many people, including my friends, neighbors, and classmates, for making my life what it is today, one of happiness and lots of fond memories of my childhood.

Two Nails

ON MAY 10, 1939, George and Lydia Evans had their seventh child—a beautiful, perfect little boy they named Roger Louis Evans. When Lydia saw her perfect little boy, she told George, "We are not having any more kids because we now have the perfect child."

That is my story and I am sticking to it, but my siblings have a different version. They say that when Dr. Carr handed me to my dad, he looked at me and said, "Lydia, that is the ugliest baby I have ever seen, and we are not having any more." I still like my version better.

Here we were, seven kids and our parents living in a three-room house with no indoor plumbing. Still, we were happy and things were going great until 1941. That's when my mother became ill, and she was committed to the West Virginia State Mental Hospital in Spencer, West Virginia. She was diagnosed with schizophrenia and would spend the next nineteen years of her life in a mental hospital. My dad was faced with raising seven kids ranging in age from two to fourteen years old. People have often asked me how my dad was able to overcome such a challenge. I would always tell them that it was with his strong faith in God and two nails. My dad had driven two nails in the wall behind the old wood-burning cookstove, and he left them sticking out about half an inch. Upon those two nails he placed two long-stem switches from his rosebush, minus the thorns. My dad was a religious man, and he believed in the old saying, "Spare the rod and spoil the child." I think it can truly be said that George Evans didn't have any spoiled children. He was practicing tough love long before it ever became a buzz word. I think that each one of us felt the pain from those switches, but I don't think we were ever punished for the same thing twice because once was enough. I know that I was born the perfect child, but I had more whippings than any of my siblings.

On a hot summer day, my brother Dennis and I and the Blankenship kids were going down to the river for a swim. A train was blocking out path to the river, and it was still in the process of switching rail cars. We couldn't wait so we crawled under the rail car and went on to the swimming hole. It seems as though our sister Irene thought that it was unsafe to crawl under the train car while the engine was running, so she told our dad, and Dennis and I got our whipping.

When I was twelve years old, I thought that I needed to start smoking. Again the same sister told our dad, and again he grabbed one of the switches from those two nails. He started whipping me, and we began going round and around in the living room. He told me, "Son, this hurts me more than it does you." I replied, "Well, Dad, you take it easy on yourself." That was sixty-five years ago, and I have never had the habit of smoking. Who needs the patch? I don't need the stinking patch. I think that when Dad was giving me that whipping as we danced around the living room, I learned how to do all kinds of new dance steps. Heck, I was doing the twist long before Chubby Checker was ever born.

Somehow we all managed to get through those hard times, and all seven kids graduated from Big Creek High School. Dad couldn't afford to send us to college, so all five of the boys went into the Air Force and used the GI Bill to attend college. One of my sisters also attended college, so six of the seven kids did have some college education. My dad's name was never listed in *Forbes* magazine as one of the richest men in the world, but if ever there was a list of fathers who were most loved and respected by his kids, I think that the name George W. Evans would be at the top. We owe him so much for keeping us all together after our mother was hospitalized.

She was released from the hospital in 1960, and my dad retired from the Norfolk & Western Railroad Company after working for forty-seven years. He and Mother moved to Michigan in 1964 to be near all seven of their kids. We all lived within a twenty-five-mile radius of Ypsilanti, Michigan. After moving to Michigan, my dad did volunteer work with mentally retarded kids at the Ypsilanti State Hospital. He and my mother were married for sixty-three years when he passed away in 1988 at the age of eighty-eight, and my mother passed away two years later. Both are truly missed and loved by the remaining five kids; two of my brothers also have passed away.

My adult life has paralleled that of my dad's in so many ways. I am thankful for the lessons I learned as I was growing up in McDowell County and to have had my dad as an example for what a father should be. I married Denise Legault in 1962, and we were blessed with three beautiful kids. Things were going great and life was good until 1968 when Denise started getting very depressed. She was admitted to a mental hospital in Ann Arbor, Michigan. She was diagnosed as manic-depressive, and later that terminology would be changed to bi-polar. Just like my dad, I was left with three kids to raise, and our youngest was only one and a half years old at that time. I was lucky that Mother and Dad were able to stay with my kids while I was at work, and for the most part, Denise would spend four to six weeks in the hospital until they could get her medication corrected. She was hospitalized thirty-four times until her death in 2014. Each time Denise needed to be hospitalized, I would always think about my dad and what he went through for nineteen years without his wife by his side. Each time Denise had to go back to the hospital I would think, "Is this the time that she will be there for the rest of her life?" Just like my dad, my three kids and I were able to get things done around the house and take care of Denise at the same time. I thank God every day for our three kids helping me take care of their mother, and now that Denise has passed away, I need my kids more than ever. Without them I don't think that I could have made it.

People have asked me if I was angry with God because my mother was in a mental hospital for nineteen years and that my wife had been in and out of a mental hospital for forty-five years. I guess I could be angry, but I choose not to be. I like to think that the things that I learned from watching my mother and dad have helped me understand the problems that Denise had to face every day of her life. Sometimes I feel that God had prepared me and chose me to take care of Denise. I know that

I could not have done it without the lessons that I learned from watching my dad as he took care of my mother.

My childhood was shaped by the love of my dad and those two nails in the wall behind the cookstove. So too has my adult life been molded by two nails—the two nails that were driven into the hands of Jesus as he lay on the cross.

Lydia and George Evans with their seven kids and their spouses, when we were all living in Michigan 1984. This is the last picture taken of the whole family together.

This is Excelsior, West Virginia where I was born and my story began seventy seven years ago.

Mother Is Coming Home

THIS IS MY story about growing up in the hills of West Virginia and how it shaped my life. My name is Roger Evans and I was the last and seventh child of Lydia and George Evans. We lived in a house on the side of the mountain located above the railroad tracks and below the highway. The Norfolk & Western Railroad provided the house because my dad worked for the company and did so for forty-seven years before his retirement in 1964. I also want to tell how my life paralleled my dad's life and the adversity we faced with our wives. My dad had to raise seven kids ages two to fourteen without the help of his wife. I faced the same task with my three young kids. I hope to convey the lessons that I learned watching my dad raise us kids and would later help me in raising my own kids. This book is dedicated to my mother and dad and also to my wife, Denise. I want to include my three kids Tony, Pamela, and Gail because I don't think that I could have made it without their help, love, and support.

The First Thing
I Can Remember

WHEN I WAS five years old, I was playing football with my brother Dennis and the three Blankenship brothers, Clarence, Ernest and Wayne. We were playing a game called "Whoever Gets the Ball Eats Dirt." I don't think that it was an official game back then but one that we had made up, and the only rule was to get the football and then run like hell before the other kids tackled you and made you eat dirt. I don't know if I was the fastest kid, but I did get to the football first. I didn't pick it up and run with it but just fell on it like I was recovering a fumble. I was lying on the ball with my two legs bent at the knees, and the other four boys jumped on top of me and tried to get the football. When they fell on top of me, I heard something snap like a dry twig. I started crying and yelling that my leg was broken. The four guys jumped up and took off running to their houses and left me lying there crying.

I don't remember how we got to the hospital in Welch, West Virginia, because my dad didn't own a car. It was a badly broken leg, and I was put in a cast from my waistline down to the tip of my toes. I had to lie in the hospital bed with my leg raised up with a rope that was anchored to the ceiling. This is where I spent the next six weeks of my life. Because I was a five-year-old, snot-nosed, crying kid, my oldest brother, Walter, who was seventeen at that time, had to stay with me. He liked to draw satirical cartoons commenting on the political matters of that time and had a notebook full of drawings he completed while he was babysitting his five-year-old brother. Walt's oldest daughter, Chatrina, had all of her dad's drawings, and she gave me one of them he had drawn for me in a frame. It is seventy-two years later, and every time I look at the picture, I think about my brother and how hard it must have been for him to sit in the hospital and watch his five-year-old, snot-nosed brother. I know when I was seventeen, I had other things on my mind. Walter would go on to be a very important influence in my life.

After six weeks in the hospital and another two weeks at home, I had to return to the hospital so the cast could be removed from my leg. Once it had been removed, I couldn't stand up on my leg and had to learn how to walk again. My biggest problem was fear, fear of falling and breaking it again. As time passed, things improved and I was back running and playing like it had never happened. Now it was time for me to get ready to start the first grade. We didn't have a kindergarten class back in our school system in the fall of 1945.

My First Day of School

I CAN STILL remember my first day of school and what an embarrassment it turned out to be. We lived in the small town of War, West Virginia, and everyone in town knew all or most of the other residents. So the schoolteachers also knew just about everyone in town and often ended up t eaching all the kids in the same family, as did Mrs. Brown who had all seven of the Evans kids. Mrs. Shelly, my first grade teacher, wanted to know who our parents were. She went down each row and asked each kid, "What is the name of your mother and father?" When she got to me, she asked, "What is your father's name?" I told her, "My dad's name is George Evans." Then she asked me my mother/s name. "My mother's name is Big Mommy," I replied, and the entire class started laughing as my face turned bright red. Mrs. Shelly asked me to talk with my dad and find out what my mother's name was.

When I got home and we were eating supper, Big Mommy asked me how my first day of school was. I told her that I didn't like school because all the kids in my class laughed at me. She asked me why they had laughed at me. I told her that my teacher asked what my mother's name was and I said Big Mommy. Big Mommy starting laughing and said, "Honey, I am not your mother; I am your grandmother." She was my dad's mother, and as long as I could remember, she had lived with us. She was called Big Mommy so I thought she was my mother.

Then I was told that my mother was in a mental hospital in Spencer, West Virginia. To a five-year-old kid back in 1945, I had no clue what a mental hospital was used for. My brothers and sisters told me that Mother had a mental illness. That meant nothing to me because I couldn't understand it. I learned that Mother was committed to the hospital in 1941 when I was just two years old. She was diagnosed as schizophrenic with psychotic symptoms. Back then the medical field knew very little about this type of mental illness, and she was given what they called the "ice pick" operation. They drilled a hole in the top of her head to clip a nerve that they thought was causing her to be violent. They also clipped the optic nerve by mistake, which left her legally blind. These are things that I discovered years later. In the mind of a five-year-old kid, I was still trying to understand what mental illness was. I went back to school the next day and was proud to tell Mrs. Shelly that my mother's name was Lydia Evans.

Mental Illness, Now I Know

WE DIDN'T HAVE a car and there were no school buses for the War Grade School, so we had to walk about a mile to school. We always walked along the railroad tracks to and from school. One morning, as we were walking to school, about six of us kids together came upon a black lady sitting on the ground with her legs crossed and an apron over her dress. She was sitting there singing while she pulled the grass and placed it on her apron. There was also some other type of green leaves that she was pulling and placing on her apron. Then she began eating the green leaves and grass she had picked. I don't remember who in our group of kids said, "Don't pay any attention to her; she suffers from mental illness."

So now I was starting to understand what my mother was like, but this was still the thinking of a five-year-old kid. Back in 1945 a five-year-old kid did not have a TV, a computer, or a smartphone to help increase his or her knowledge about the world. All we knew was what was happening on our side of the mountain. Today I am glad that we didn't have all those things because we were always playing in the mountains or fishing down by the river. These were the mountains that I loved and would spend the next thirteen years of my life enjoying before leaving West Virginia to joint the Air Force.

Hillside Hotshots

LIVING ON THE side of a mountain, we didn't have any flat ground to play basketball. Dennis and I talked with Clarence, Ernest, and Wayne about making a flat area where we could put up a basketball net and have a place to play. With our pick and shovels in hand, we went about a hundred yards from our houses and started digging out the side of the mountain. After three weeks and a lot of digging and leveling of the ground, we had a place to play basketball. Now all we needed was to install a basketball net. I don't know where we got it, but we found one, so we got scrap wood from anywhere we could find it and put together a backboard. Then we attached the rim to the backboard. We cut a tree so we could attach the backboard to it, dug a hole, and installed our basketball net. We were ready to play. All summer long if we were not up in the mountains playing, we were playing basketball. The only downside to our new basketball court was that if you lost a ball out of bounds, it would roll all the way down to the bottom of the hill, or as Clarence would say to Wayne, "Go down in the holler and get the ball."

After playing all summer we thought we were getting pretty good, so we needed someone to compete with. We went down in Excelsior bottom and challenged some black kids, who were friends of ours. We played on their court because they had two basketball nets. We found out quickly that we were not as good as we thought we were. We climbed back up the hill with our tails tucked between our legs. We said, "Just wait until fall; we will kick their butts in football." We no longer called ourselves the Hillside Hotshots, but we knew we could beat them in football. Just wait!

Fly Away

ABOVE OUR HOUSE at the top of the mountain was a large rock cliff and it was above the tree line. In the summertime we spent many hours on top of the rock cliff. It was a good place to view the valley, the river, and the railroad tracks. Back in those days, there were many trains hauling coal to places unknown to us. Most of the kids I went to school with had dads who worked in the coal mines. My dad and his two brothers and their dad all worked on the railroad. Clarence, Ernest, Wayne, Dennis, and I would climb on top of the rock cliff carrying a catalog with us so we could make paper airplanes and sail them off the mountain. Our goal was to try to get one all the way down to the river. I don't remember any of us reaching that goal; it was a very long way to the river. I used to sit up there sailing paper airplanes and daydream about someday being a pilot so I could fly over the top of the mountain on the other side of the valley. I had always wanted to see the other side. Sitting up on top of that big rock cliff gave me such a good feeling; it made me feel like I was closer to God. Looking back on it now makes me think that God was with us while we were playing because we never had any accidents. If we had, we were sure to die because it was a long fall, and more than likely we would land on the large rocks at the bottom of the cliff. Even if we were not sailing paper airplanes from the top of the cliff, we would go up there and just sit, looking out over the valley and thinking about where we would be in twenty years.

At that time we never had any thoughts of ever leaving West Virginia, but the coal mines were slowing down and that was about the only place to work for the people who chose to stay in the area. Lots of people from our area left and went to Detroit, Michigan, to get jobs in the auto factories. That is where all of my family would end up. There is an old saying, "You can take the boy out of the country, but you can't take the country out of the boy." That is so true. I still love the mountains and wish I could go back to the top of the rock cliff and fly away.

McDowell County, West Virginia

MCDOWELL COUNTY, WEST Virginia, is the most southern county in the state. It is on the border of Virginia. Most of the people living in McDowell County earned their living working in the coal mines. The owners of the coal mines provided houses for their employees, owned the general store, and provided doctors and dentists for all of the coal camps. The employees bought most of their needs from the company store and took their kids to the company doctor or company dentist, Most of the miners did owe their soul to the company store. The Norfolk & Western Railroad also provided houses for their employees but on a much smaller scale. The pay was also much lower than what the coal miners earned.

On the hillside where I was born, there were four houses built for the railroad workers. Our house was just below the highway; it was a three-room house with no indoor plumbing. When I was born, Dr. Carr came to the house to deliver the perfect little boy for Lydia and George Evans. The cost for that house call and delivery was twenty-five dollars, but my dad didn't have that much money so he paid Dr. Carr whenever he could. That was true with anything that my dad would buy; he didn't have the money so it was put on a tab, and he would pay a couple dollars a month until it was paid in full. That was one of the good things about growing up in McDowell County; people trusted you and would help you any way they could.

As a kid growing up there, you had better not do anything wrong because your dad would know it when you got home. I never understood how he knew so quickly because we didn't have a phone. In our three-room house, we had a kitchen and two bedrooms with an outhouse. In those two bedrooms you had to have space for nine people to sleep, so most of the time there were three or four people in each bed, depending on the size of the kids. We were poor, but we never knew that because most of the families were in the same condition. McDowell County was a great place to grow up.

*One of the many steam engine trains that hauled coal out of
McDowell County, WVA.*

The Gang of Five

DENNIS AND I, along with the Blankenship brothers, no longer called our gang "the Hillside Hotshots after the thrashing we got in basketball from the black kids down in Excelsior bottom. We were now the "Gang of Five." We were together every day planning a camping trip up in the mountains, down on the river bank fishing, or just hanging out and making some new toys to use. We didn't have any money so we had to make toys to play with. We made slingshots, using a forked stick with bicycle inner-tube rubber and a shoe tongue to hold the ammunition. Most of the ammunition was used for hunting lizards, and once in a while we shot at a hornet's nest, I never said that we were the smartest kids in McDowell County.

We also made our own bow and arrows, using a sapling strung with battery wire and stick weed for the arrows. One time we were on top of Sunshine Ridge with our bow and arrows, and we decided to have a game and try to shoot each other. Ernest was hiding behind a tree and stuck his head out to locate someone to shoot. I was too late because Clarence had already spotted him and let an arrow fly. The arrow ended up stuck in Ernest's lip and left a hole in it, which made it difficult to drink water. There was always a bunch of old scrap cars around, and we used a hacksaw to cut the roofs off to use as floating boats.

There were so many other toys that we made, such as boats, sleds, and pistols. We would also dig up different kinds of roots to sell and make money so we could sneak off to the movies every Saturday. The biggest money-making root that we dug up was ginseng, but we also dug snakeroot and mayapple root. The Gang of Five was busy all the time entertaining ourselves. We never heard of, nor did we knowing the meaning of, the word *bored*.

Big Mommy's Passing

IN 1949, WHEN I was ten years old, it was the first time I had to deal with a death in our family. Big Mommy had been living with us for the last seven years, and on a very cold December morning, I can remember seeing her take her last breath as she lay in her bed. She'd had a heart attack. She was born in 1870 and passed away in 1949 at the age of seventy-nine. At this point in my life she was the only mother figure I knew. I don't know why she was called Big Mommy because she was small in stature, about five foot five, and weighed about 104 pounds. She always wore an apron over her long dress, and in her apron pockets she had some Mickey Twist chewing tobacco and some Birch Bark twigs. She wasn't like a baseball player with a big chew of tobacco in her jaw, but she used just a small amount in her mouth, and afterward she spit it out and used the birch bark twigs to refresh her mouth. She was a very hard worker and did most of the cooking, and she made sure that all of us kids had chores to do every day. Some were assigned to making the beds; others had the chore of doing dishes. Dennis and I had the responsibility of getting the firewood. Most of the firewood was from old railroad ties. Most of the cooking in those days was the same every day: biscuits and gravy with some type of pork meat for breakfast, and for supper it was pinto beans, fried potatoes, and cornbread. On Sunday we had fried chicken with biscuits and gravy for our supper. We didn't have things like a toaster, mixer, or any other kitchen aid to help make cooking easier. If we wanted toast, we had to butter the bread on one side, put it in a bread pan with the buttered side up, and stick it in the oven until the sides turned brown. Before you did that, you had to make sure you had a fire going in the old wood and coal cookstove.

Big Mommy taught us all how to make quilts using our old clothes; bib overalls were the most common material used. We cut the material into square patches and sewed them together. She also taught us how to make pillows using the feathers we had plucked from the chicken we killed for our Sunday supper. Big Mommy was always busy sewing our torn clothes on the old Singer foot-petal sewing machine. I think back on her life and know that it must have been hard at her age to do all the things that she did for us, but never do I remember her complaining. She was strong in her faith, and when we did something wrong, she quoted something from the Bible to try to set us on the straight and narrow path to a good life. Big Mommy was in charge of the Maytag washing machine because she was afraid that one of the smaller kids would get their hands caught in the ringers, as so many kids did back in those days. We didn't have a dryer, so the clothes were hung outside on a clothesline, which didn't work so well on those cold winter days.

I was ten years old when Big Mommy passed, and what made it worse was after they took her body away, she was brought back to our three-room house in her casket for the wake, which was held in one of the bedrooms. It didn't give me a good feeling, having a dead person in my bedroom for two days. I don't think I got very much sleep. She was buried next to her husband, who had passed away eleven years earlier. I missed Big Mommy (Matilda Jane Evans) because she was the only mother that I knew. I am sure I am who I became because of the values she instilled in me. She was a very kind and gentle soul.

After her passing our chores were increased to make up for what she had been doing. My dad was cooking our breakfast, working from the same menu of biscuits and gravy that continued for the next eight years until I joined the Air Force. Don't get me wrong; I am not complaining about the menu because I could still eat the same breakfast seven days a week like we did back then, but that may also explain why I have so many doctor's appointments today.

Big Mommy (Matilda Jane Evans), born in 1870 and passed in 1949. The only mother I ever knew.

Rolling Rocks
and Forest Fires

I THINK THAT I was about twelve years old when these events happened. Above the highway and up the holler lived the Belcher family just a short distance from our house. Edgel and Rosie Belcher had three kids, Edgel Jr., Sue, and Raymond. They were in the same age bracket as the Gang of Five, and on this day we were all up on top of the mountain. One of our made-up games was to see who could roll a rock down the mountainside for the longest distance. If you got the rock with the best shape for rolling, you could claim the prize, which was just the bragging rights until we had another rock-rolling contest. We were right above the Belchers' house but just a little bit to the east of it. Rosie was in the yard doing their washing. The Belchers didn't own a washing machine, so Rosie used a washtub situated on some rocks with a fire under it to heat up the water for a cleaner wash. Her husband drove a coal truck, but he still had lots of coal dust on his clothes, so she needed the water to get hot to remove the coal dust. All seven of us kids were doing okay with the rolling rocks, and someone got a rock rolling so fast that it continued on its path toward the washtub.

Rosie was out there near the washtub with a stick, stirring the clothes, and she heard a loud noise. She looked up and saw the big rock tumbling down the mountain at a fast clip. Rosie threw her stick down and ran into the house just as the big rock smashed into the washtub. The Gang of Five took a different route to get back to our homes so we wouldn't have to face Rosie. We could hear her yelling at Junior and Raymond as they got back to their house.

Think it was late March, and the Gang of Five was up in the mountains. We had just finished a lunch of hot dogs cooked over an open fire with some warmed-up pork and beans. We were sitting around the fire, picking our teeth with birch bark twigs, when someone came up with the idea that we should practice our fire-fighting skills. We had done this many times. We would rake up a pile of dry leaves, set them on fire, and then cut some tree branches with green leaves on them to fight the fire and put it out. No problem, we had done this before, and we knew what we were doing. The conditions on this day were very dry, and the wind was blowing at a pretty good clip. We fought the blaze for quite a while, but it looked like we were losing the battle and the flames started to encircle us. As a group, we threw our tree branches down and ran like hell all the way back to our houses. We were very frightened, and my sister Irene knew something was wrong. We wouldn't tell her what we had done, however, because we were afraid that she would tell our dad. That would mean a good whipping, and we'd already had some of those because Irene would tell on us for things that we had done like smoking. Irene said that she wouldn't tell Dad because this was such a big fire and it burned for almost two weeks before the rain put it out. If we had been caught for starting the forest fire, we may have been sent to a reform school. Back in the mountains, it was almost impossible to put out forest fires because you couldn't get any equipment up in the mountains to fight the fire. I don't recall if the fire caused any houses to burn down, but there were very few houses that high on the mountainside because there were no roads going up to the top. If there was any one thing that I could change about our childhood, this would be the one thing. We loved the mountains, and we meant no harm to anyone or any of the animals that had to leave because of our mistake. Out of the Gang of Five, none of us became fire fighters because our careers took different directions.

Two Sisters

THERE WERE FIVE boys and two girls in our family, and to this day I don't know how my dad was able to keep his family together after our mother was committed to a mental hospital. His strong faith in God and his love for each one of his kids played a big role in keeping us all together; of this I am sure. We became a very close family because of what we went through as we were growing up in McDowell County, West Virginia. Being the youngest of the seven kids, I feel that I owe each one of them so much for keeping me in line. When Mother was taken away, my oldest brother, Walter, was fourteen years old, Robert was twelve, Jerry ten, Betty eight, Irene six, Dennis four, and I was two years old. Because of our ages, each one of the kids has a different memory of the day Mother was taken away. This was something that was never talked about as a family, but because Walter was fourteen years old at the time, I am sure he could remember everything that happened that day. I am also sure that Robert, Jerry, Betty, and Irene can also remember that day. I was two years old so I had nothing to overcome, but I am sure that my siblings each had their own memories to deal with. After Mother was taken away, my dad's mother came to live with us, and for the next seven years, she became our mother. In those seven years she taught each one of us so many different things about life. My two sisters needed a mother figure around more so than the boys.

Some of my first memories are of Betty rocking me to sleep in the old handmade rocking chair. I can also remember sucking my thumb and curling my hair; that lasted until the third grade. I was hoping that I could quit before I got into high school. After Big Mommy passed away, Betty became my mother figure. When my leg was broken and in a full cast, I can remember Betty carrying me to school with her for a day; it must have been close to a mile that we walked to school. My other sister, Irene, may have been a mother to Dennis and me, but I think you could say that she was the mother of discipline. She was the reason Dennis and I got more whippings than any of the other siblings. I used to think that Big Mommy must have been giving Irene just a small pinch of her Mickey Twist chewing tobacco each time that Irene turned us in for something we had done wrong. I was so thankful that she didn't turn us in when we started the forest fire. The only reason she didn't was because it was such a big fire that she was afraid we would be sent off to Punnytown, the reform school for boys. If we were in reform school, she and Betty would have to cut all the firewood for cooking and heating the house.

Betty and Irene both played a big part in my growing up and keeping me on the straight and narrow. Just a few years ago I wrote both of them a letter to say how much I owed them for helping to raise me and how much I loved them. I had to tell them in a letter because I would have cried if I tried to do it in person. I sit here today and think how each one of my siblings contributed so much to my upbringing. I have a great family and a lot of love for my two sisters.

Peking Duck

WHEN WE WERE growing up in McDowell County, we were very poor, but we didn't know that because most of our neighbors were just like us. We didn't need money to buy toys because we made our own and entertained ourselves. We also never ate in a restaurant that served Peking duck, so this is how we had our first opportunity to eat that delicacy. Dennis, Clarence, Ernest, Wayne, and I—the Gang of Five—had been fishing, and when the fish stopped biting, we started skipping rocks across the river. Just as the sun was going down behind the distant mountain, we noticed on the opposite shore Mrs. Goforth's favorite egg-laying duck sitting on its nest. Faster than you could say "Jackie Robinson," we switched from skipping stones to chucking rocks at that duck. About that time Mrs. Goforth saw what we were doing, and she began yelling at us. Even though she was a member of the Rosebud Baptist Church, it was times like this that would cause her to lose her religion and use cuss words that even Satan wouldn't use. Even the cuss words couldn't save that duck as one of the rocks found its mark—one broken neck and that was one dead duck. Ernest ran across the river and picked up the dead duck, and we were off to our favorite hideout. When we reached the highway, we could still hear Mrs. Goforth cussing us for killing her egg-laying duck.

Just above the highway was a rock cliff we called Man Head, and it was one of our favorite places to hang out. By this time it was starting to get dark, so Ernest, Wayne, and I gathered some firewood as Dennis and Clarence plucked the feathers from the duck, gutting it and cleaning it up as best they could with no water to wash it out. Clarence was the oldest, so he was put in charge of the cooking. He cut a sapling branch, stuck it through the duck, and put it over the fire. He rotated the duck to make sure it was cooked to perfection. By this time it was very dark, and we didn't have flashlights with us to check to see if the duck was done. Clarence said that the duck was done, so he pulled his Swiss Army knife from his pocket and began cutting it into five pieces. We sat around the fire eating our fine Peking duck, and all you could hear was the crackling of the fire and lips smacking as we enjoyed our duck, the juice running down our chins. After the fine dinner, we pulled some birch twigs from our pockets that we always carried. Not only were they used as toothpicks but the sweet flavor of the birch twigs also served as an after-dinner mint. As the last embers of the fire flicked out, we found our way back to our houses.

When we walked into our house, Irene had a look of fear on her face. She told us to go look at ourselves in the mirror. That wasn't duck juice running down our chin; it was duck blood. Seems as though the head chef, Clarence, didn't cook it as long as he should have. I don't know why we let Clarence be in charge of the cooking because when he was younger, he made biscuits and gravy for us; the biscuits were not too bad, but we couldn't eat his gravy. Since we couldn't eat the gravy, he gave it to his dog. His dog ate some, and it tasted so bad that he licked his butt to take the taste out of his mouth. Today, when I go into a restaurant that has duck on the menu, it takes me back to the Peking duck we enjoyed so much while we were growing up in McDowell County. Yes, we were poor, but I wouldn't trade my childhood for anything and all the memories we had growing up with the Blankenship kids. They were great neighbors.

The Holidays

BACK IN THE 1940s, Christmas was our special holiday but not because we got lots of gifts; we didn't get many toys. It was a time when we still believed in Santa Claus. About a month before Christmas we were on our best behavior because we didn't want to get a lump of coal in our hanging stockings. Christmas was also the time of year that we got new school clothes, mail-ordered from Montgomery Ward. The Blankenship kids got their clothes ordered from Sears & Roebuck, and we envied them because we hated Montgomery Ward. The biggest Christmas gift that I can remember getting was a Lionel electric train set that Dennis and I shared. I also remember when Irene got a doll that had hair. I was still sucking my thumb and curling my hair, so I started curling her doll's hair and it wasn't long before the doll had no hair. Needless to say, Irene wasn't happy. The holiday was also special because of the Christmas tree. The old railroad house we lived in had a twelve-foot-high ceiling. We would go up in the mountains to find a tree that was suitable for our house, and most of the time the tree top would touch the ceiling when we stood it up inside the house.

Most of the decorations were handmade by us kids. We made paper chains, and because we had no glue or tape to connect each link in the chain, we made paste out of flour and water. We also used popcorn and thread it with a needle to connect each one of the popped kernels to make a chain. Then we draped it around the tree. We had a few ornaments and some green-and-red rope chains that were used each year to help decorate the tree. Christmas was special for all of the kids growing up back in those days, and we were taught the reason for the season.

Thanksgiving

THANKSGIVING WAS ALSO a special day, not just because of the great dinner of turkey and homemade stuffing with all the other trimmings, but for us young boys it was the time for killing the hogs. Every spring our dad bought baby pigs and put them in the hog pen made out of railroad ties. We would feed them so they would be ready for slaughter about Thanksgiving time. Those hogs would be our meat for the winter. It was an exciting time for the young boys in our family, plus the Blankenship boys, because we got to help with the process. We would dig a hole in the ground and on one side make about a forty-five-degree slant so that a fifty-five-gallon barrel would fit in it. Then we'd fill the barrel with water and build a fire under it to bring the water to a boil so the pig could be submerged in the hot water after it was shot and killed. Submerging the pig in the hot water made it easier to scrape off its hair. After the cleaning process was done, the butchering process began. Everything on the pig was used; nothing went to waste. The intestines, ears, feet, and tail were given to the Pennington family, who lived below us at the bottom of the hill. Dennis, Clarence, Ernest, Wayne, and I couldn't wait to get the pig's bladder. We would drain it and use a stick weed to blow air into the bladder, tie it off so the air wouldn't leak out, and begin kicking the bladder like a football. No, we didn't invent the first true pigskin football but were just making the most out of our situation at that time. The experience that I received by helping my Dad with the butchering process would help me later in life when I started deer hunting and doing the butchering with my brothers. Thanksgiving was truly a special day because we were very thankful for the food on our table.

The Fourth of July

THE FOURTH OF July was also a special day of celebration for us younger kids. There were many games to participate in, and we had the usual fireworks display. As a kid you didn't want to wear your best clothes because they wouldn't look the same at the end of the day. We had a greased pig contest in which a pig was greased up and all the kids formed a circle around the pig. When the pig was released, we tried to pick it up; if we were able to do that, we became the owner(s) of the pig. When the contest was over, the pig was clean but not us kids. I don't remember anyone ever catching the pig.

We also had a greased pole contest. Grease was applied to the flag pole, and the object was to see who could climb the highest on the pole. I was never a winner at this game either. The other event I liked as a kid was watching the Coon on a Log contest. All of the old coon hunters would bring their best coon-hunting dog to enter into this event. A coon was placed on a log that was floating in the water, and the dogs had to try to get the coon off of the log. The dogs would swim out to the log holding the coon, but the coon had the advantage.

A smart coon could push the dog's head under the water, and after being forced underwater a few times, the dogs would give up. I can only remember one time when I saw a dog get the log rolling until the coon fell in the water. I used to enjoy watching these events as we celebrated the Fourth of July.

Back when I was young and growing up in the mountains, times were hard, but the holidays were so special to us. We never had many material things, but we always had food on the table, and for that I am so thankful. We owed that to our hardworking and loving dad who was able to keep us all together after Mother was committed to the mental hospital.

My First Love

WHEN I WAS about eight years old and in the fourth grade, I loved my teacher, Mrs. Whit, but my first true love happened later in the year. A new girl moved into the town of War from Bartley, another coal mining camp located just a few miles down the road. When she came into the classroom, Mrs. Whit introduced her to the rest of the students and placed her in the seat just in front of me. From the moment that this girl walked into our class, I couldn't take my eyes off of her. She was a small girl with short dark hair, big brown eyes, a very cute face, and a quirky smile. For the rest of the day, I don't think that I heard anything that Mrs. Whit was trying to teach us because I couldn't take my eyes off of the new girl in our class.

I couldn't wait for the next school day so I could see the love of my life. I don't know if it was because I put too much sugar in the cornflakes I had for breakfast that morning or just the sight of the new girl in our class, but it seems as though my heart was beating faster than normal. That very cute girl with the quirky smile was Sandy Counts, who would later be selected as the most humorous in the graduating class of 1957.

Sandy never knew that she was my first love until one of our class reunions when I let her know that she was my first true love. We remained friends all through grade school, junior high, and high school, and she was still a very beautiful person when we graduated. Back in the fourth grade, I couldn't talk to Sandy because I loved her, and I didn't know anything about love. I didn't have my mother so I didn't have anyone to teach me about love. Without his wife, my dad couldn't display any emotion of love as an example for his kids. Growing up, we knew that our dad loved us, but he could never express himself and let us know how he felt. It must have been very hard for him to raise seven kids without the help of his wife. Later on in my life, I would learn how it feels to raise your kids without your wife; I think you could say I walked a mile in his shoes. So much to learn about love, but Sandy was my first.

I Am Sorry

I THINK I was in the fourth grade as I was walking home from school one day along the railroad tracks. I came to the point where I had to follow the path up the hillside to our house. In doing so, I had to walk through the yard of the Penningtons, and Buddy Pennington was a black friend of the Gang of Five. Buddy spent a lot of time playing with us at our house, and it seemed that he was with us just about every Sunday because he knew that we would have fried chicken for supper. He loved fried chicken, and by the time he got finished with a chicken leg, there was nothing left on it; even the dogs didn't want the chicken bone. As I was going through Buddy's yard, some of his toys were lying in the sand, so I picked up a fire truck and a toy car and proceeded up the hill to my house. I played with them for a couple of days before my dad noticed the new toys I had collected. He asked me where I had gotten those toys, and I had to tell him that I had picked them up in Buddy's yard as I came home from school. He made me pick up those toys and then walked me down the hill to Buddy's house. I had to knock on the door, and although Buddy wasn't at home, his dad was. I stood there shaking in my shoes as I gave the toys back to Mr. Pennington. I had to tell him that I was sorry for stealing Buddy's toys. I can't remember what, if anything, Mr. Pennington said, but he knew my dad very well and our home situation. He probably thought that my dad was trying to teach me a valuable lesson in life.

I was very surprised that I didn't get a whipping, but Dad's method worked because that was the end of my career as a thief. I can't count the times that the Gang of Five would be up in the mountains smoking some cigarette butts that we had picked up along the highway. Then we would go over to Mr. Childers's garden on the side of the mountain and eat some of his green onions to cover up the smoke smell on our breath. That wasn't considered stealing to us; that was just protecting our butts so we didn't get a whipping for smoking.

Movie Money

WHEN WE WERE growing up, our dad wouldn't let us go to the movies. I don't know if he thought that it was a sin or that we were so poor that we shouldn't be wasting money on the movies. When Dennis and I were about twelve and ten years old, we would sneak out and go to the movies with the Blankenship boys just about every Saturday afternoon. We would see the old cowboys and Indians movies, plus there was always a serial that ran for fifteen weeks and then another one would start. Of course we never received an allowance, so we would do many different things to get our money for the movies. One that paid good money was digging for ginseng roots, but they had to be dry or the guy wouldn't buy them. So when we found some roots to dig, we put them on the sheet metal roof of our chicken house; they would dry fast lying in the hot sun. We also dug snakeroot and mayapple root; all of these roots were used for making medication. We cut sticks for staking tomato plants in people's gardens and cut firewood for some of the older folks. We used to cut Mr. Coffee's yard with an old push-type reel mower; he had a big yard and it was a lot of hard work but good money.

Most of the houses in the area were built on the side of the mountains, and when people bought a truckload of coal, there was no way the truck could get close to the house so the coal was dumped by the roadside. People hired us to carry the coal up or down the hill and put it in their coal bin. We used burlap sacks to carry the coal on our backs to the bins. It took a lot of trips up and down the mountain to transport one ton of coal. We looked like miners when we were done, and we were just as tired as a miner after finishing his shift in the mine. After we finished hauling the coal to the bins, we got a bar of soap and a towel and headed to the river for a bath. In the wintertime we cut down big gum trees that had mistletoe growing in the top of them and also cut holly bushes and made Christmas decorations to sell. We also cut Christmas trees for people who couldn't cut their own; there was no such thing as a place to go and buy a Christmas tree. The money that we made for doing these things was a very small amount, but the cost of a ticket to see a movie was only twenty cents and popcorn was also twenty cents. So we did all right for five young boys, and we got to see lots of movies. We also spent some of that hard-earned money for an RC Cola and a bag of peanuts to put into the cola. Man, was that good! That would even taste good today.

The Seventh Grade

I WAS ABOUT eleven years old and had completed the sixth grade; now it was time for me to move on to War Junior High School. The biggest difference was that I would be changing classrooms every hour and have a different teacher for each class. That was going to take some adjustment, plus I was going out for the football and basketball teams. I was very small when I went out for the football team and really don't remember much of what happened the first year, except that I spent most of my time holding the dummies in practice .I don't remember if I ever got to play in one of our games.

When I started the seventh grade, it was the first year we would have eleven players on the football team—before that it was a six-man team—so my chances of making the team were almost double. I must have done all right the first year because Coach Payne let me come out for the second year. He was a tough coach but a very good one. He was also a tough teacher; I had him for my science class and if you failed any of his tests, he would bring you in front of the class and make you bend over and touch your toes. He had a paddle with holes in it and he would swat you on your butt. I was never on the receiving end of his so-called board of education, but watching some of the other kids made me study a little harder.

I got to play in more games when I was in the eighth grade. I was a halfback on offense and a halfback on defense; I got to carry the football and score a few touchdowns while playing on offense. I was starting to really enjoy playing football, and I had a greater interest in my basketball games too. Things were changing in my life, and I started noticing how cute the girls were. I was also gaining lots of experience in football, which I used against the black kids down in Yukon bottom. They had beaten the Hillside Hotshots badly in basketball, but we would be ready for them in our upcoming game of football.

It was a Saturday afternoon and people had gathered on a field up in Excelsior just to the east of Mr. Music's house. The black kids arrived, and we said our hellos and flipped the coin to see who would get the ball first. We won the toss, and that would be the last thing we won that day. The kickoff went to Clarence Blankenship and he ran as hard as he could, but Big Head Ed came out of nowhere and flattened Clarence. Clarence was knocked out colder than a mackerel, and he was our best player. Those black kids were just too good for us; they had Little Sammy, Big Head Ed, Slim Jim, and the rest of the team. Little Sammy went on to be an all-state player from Excelsior High School and played football in college. He was very small and very fast; I believe he was Barry Sanders before Barry Sanders was even born. He was good. I think that our football game with the black kids from Yukon bottom was a big win for them, forty-eight to six, and I am still trying to figure out how we got six points.

The War Junior High School football team was doing all right. We were winning more games than we lost. The next year I would be in the ninth grade, and it looked like we would have a good year. Some of the boys that I can remember playing with were Art Pruett, Roger Gates, Dave Roberts, Glen Jesse, John Bowling, Glen Pruett, Dick Shaw, Warren Williams, and Cecil Hampton. Some of these players from War Junior High School would go on to be big stars at Big Creek High School. The next year would be my last year in junior high school, and some big changes were about to take place in my life, changes that I resisted at first. But as it turned out, it was a very good move for me.

Before my move from Excelsior, we had a score to settle with the black kids in sports. They had beaten us in basketball and trounced us in football, but we still had a chance to try our luck in baseball. We recruited some of the bigger white kids down in Excelsior bottom for our team. We had played other white kids from up in Warrior Mine holler and had beaten them. So we thought that we might be able to beat the black kids in Yukon; some of their players were the same ones who had beaten us in basketball and football. Our ball field was a big flat area that at one time had been the site of a tipple installation for processing coal. The tipple had been removed, and all that was left was a flat surface covered in coal dust and slag. The best thing about playing baseball there was our main swimming hole was just beyond the outfield, so we would all go swimming after the game. We played many games against the black kids, and we did manage to beat them. They had home field advantage because the hillside was like an amphitheater and all of the houses belonged to black families. When we played the black kids, every front porch was filled with eight or ten people from each house. When one of the black kids did something special, you could hear a big cheer coming from the hillside. Big Head Ed was a good hitter, and sometimes he would hit the ball so far that it would end up in the river. The game would be halted until we retrieved the ball because we only had one ball. We played many games with the black kids, but I don't remember who won the most. I was just glad that we found a game that we could win against them once in a while.

After the game was over, we all went swimming, and many times we swam in the nude because we didn't have our swimsuits with us. We were taking a bath more than we were swimming, and there were always the guys who were well endowed who would get out of the water and walk along the riverbank, striding like a peacock. Most of the time it was the black kids; me, I was out in the deep water. Clarence Blankenship always called these guys "bank walkers."

Moonshine Still

IN THE MOUNTAINS of southern West Virginia, moonshine was still common. The Gang of Five knew where one of these existed, and we would go up there to check it out. We never did any damage to it, nor did we ever try to drink any of the moonshine. One of our neighbors who lived down in Excelsior bottom ran the still. Boots was his name and he worked in the mines, but his moonshine business got to be a full-time job, so he quit working in the coal mines. All of the material to build this moonshine still had to be carried by hand up the mountainside. The material consisted of tubs, copper tubing, and glass jugs, plus all of the material for making the moonshine, which included corn and sugar. He collected rainwater to use in the process. Boots used to have my brother Dennis and Clarence Blankenship buy lots of sugar for him, and then Boots would buy them an RC Cola with a bag of peanuts as their pay. Lord have mercy, it just doesn't get any better than having an RC Cola and pouring a bag of peanuts in it to drink. Those were the days.

Just climbing up the mountainside was a difficult task, but

when you had to carry all of these supplies up the mountain, it became much harder. Boots had some of his boys help him get all of the supplies up to the moonshine still. One day the Gang of Five was playing up in the mountains and we decided to check out the moonshine still. You had to be very quiet as you approached the area where the still was located because when Boots was working there, he always had his rifle with him. We got close enough to see that Boots wasn't working so went over to check it out. When we got to the still, Boots had a batch that had not yet finished processing. One of the washtubs was filled with corn mash that was in the fermenting stage. Floating on top of the corn mash was a large rat. I guess it had gotten in there, got drunk, couldn't get back out, and drowned. I can almost assure you that Boots didn't throw that batch of corn mash out, but some of his customers had some moonshine with a little added protein.

The Ninth Grade

THE SUMMER BETWEEN the eighth and ninth grade was a long and hot one. So the Gang of Five spent most of its days down on the river, fishing in the morning and swimming in the afternoon. It was late summer and the leaves were turning color. There was also a smell in the air because it was time for football season to begin. I didn't need too much conditioning to prepare for the upcoming football practices that were held in the dog days of summer. We lived on the side of the mountain and didn't own a car, so I was in the best condition of my life. We had to walk everywhere we were going up and down the hill, to and from our house, to get where we were going.

Although I was in perfect condition, practice was needed to get our timing down and to work on our plays. We would put on our football uniforms, and then Coach Payne would make us run up to the practice field. We ran along the railroad tracks up to Big Creek High School's practice field. The coaches rode in their car and monitored the team as we ran. Occasionally we heard the car horn blow and one of the coaches yell at us to speed it up. We also had to run back the same route after football practice was over; it had to be over a mile each way.

All the hard work paid off because we won most of our games, and we were down to the last game of the season against Bartley Junior High, which also had a very good year. We were leading fourteen to thirteen late in the fourth quarter. I was a defensive halfback and let their end get behind me; he caught a pass and ran it in for a touchdown to win the game. I started running around to find a rock to crawl under because I felt like crap. Well, the football season was over, and now I was practicing for my final year of basketball at War Junior High. During the football season, most of the players were getting into girls, and we had a party at someone's house just about every Saturday night. I met a beautiful girl named Annette; I guess you could say that we were girlfriend and boyfriend. I think that she was the first girl I ever kissed. I can't remember who initiated that first kiss, me or her, but it was great. There were many more kisses that followed with her before the big move that was about to take place in my life.

Because of my dad's job, we were going to move to Atwell, West Virginia, which was located about twelve to fifteen miles from Excelsior, where we lived. We would be moving away from the Blankenships, who had been our best friends all of our lives. I would also be going to another junior high school, Bartley Junior High—the school that beat us in football because of my mistake. How could I ever face the kids in this new school?

We were in the middle of the basketball season, and I had played about four games at War Junior High before we moved. On my first day at Bartley, one of the teachers took me around to show me where each of my classes were, and after the classes were over, I went to the gym to talk with Coach Crisco to see if he would let me join the team. I had brought my shoes and shorts just in case he let me join the team. He told me to get dressed, and that was the beginning of my basketball days at Bartley Junior High. Remember that when I lived in Excelsior, we used to play the black kids in all sports, so I played a different style of basketball from what Coach Crisco was teaching. The black kids in Excelsior had dribbled the ball between their legs and behind their back, and they made passes without looking at their teammates. I had picked up some of those tricks and tried to play like the black kids. Coach Crisco, after watching me dribble the ball and shoot layups, put me on the first team in our scrimmage practice. I got a rebound and started dribbling down the floor, and one of my teammates was out front on a fast break. Without breaking stride, I quickly one-handed a fast pass to him without looking and caught him off guard, and the ball landed flush on his nose. His nose started bleeding, and Coach Crisco blew the whistle to stop the practice so he could take care of the player and clean up the floor. Coach Crisco came over to me and asked where I had learned to pass like that. As it turned out, the guy that I hit in the nose with the basketball was the same guy who got behind me to catch the game-winning touchdown in football when I was playing for War Junior High. I think that this is called poetic justice. I was lucky to have some good basketball players on the Bartley team. Among them were Pete Tolley, Gary Powell, and Roger Bellamy, who would become my best friends for the rest of our school days.

I had been afraid that I wouldn't have any friends at my

new school, but being the new kid helped meet lots of girls. One of those girls was Linda; she and I were girlfriend and boyfriend for the rest of the ninth grade. She was a short girl with blue eyes, blonde hair, a very pretty face, and a smile that would melt your heart. We also had parties just about every Friday night where we would get together and play games; one of those games was Spin the Bottle. I had never played that game before, so the other kids had to explain the rules to me. Someone twisted the bottle and on the first spin it was pointing at me, so I twisted the bottle until it pointed toward a girl. We were supposed to stand up and kiss. I had kissed Annette back at War Junior High but not in front of a group. So I wasn't going to kiss this girl in front of everyone. The group decided we could go into the nearby closet, and we did. Sometimes you would spend more time in the closet, depending on the girl. I was starting to love my new school.

During the basketball season at Bartley, we started having sock-hop dances in the gym during our lunchtime. The girls sat on one side of the gym and the boys on the opposite side. The music played and about the only ones dancing were the girls. After a couple of dances, there were a few boys dancing with the girls. I didn't know how to dance, so I watched and tried to see how it was done. I was also too shy to walk all the way across the floor and ask a girl to dance with me. All of the music was for slow dancing, and it didn't look like it would be too hard to learn how to dance. Slowly more and more of the boys got out on the dance floor, and it looked like they were enjoying dancing with the girls. I was sitting and watching as this pretty blond-haired girl walked across the gym floor toward me. She stopped in front of me and asked, "Would you like to dance with me?" It felt like someone took some dental floss and tied my tongue. I didn't know what to say, so I told her that I didn't know how to dance. She said, "That's okay, I'll teach you." So I got up and she led me out on the dance floor. Patti Page was singing "The Tennessee Waltz" as I stepped on this pretty girl's toes, but I was starting to feel more relaxed and even enjoyed dancing with her. Even now if I hear "The Tennessee Waltz," it takes me back to 1953 and Ruby Williams, the pretty girl who asked me to dance with her. Thank you, Ruby, for teaching me to dance.

After basketball season was over, Coach Crisco was our track coach, and we had a few meets with some of the local junior high schools, such as War, Coalwood, and Berwind. We were never trained in the different events; he let us do what we thought was our best event. I entered the half-mile race and did okay in most of my races. Then Coach Crisco entered us in a very big track meet in Beckley, West Virginia, with about forty schools from all of southern West Virginia. It was an all-day event held on a Saturday, and it was a long ride over to Beckley. When we arrived, I had never seen this many kids at a track meet, and now it was time to start the half-mile race. I think there must have been forty-five kids entered in this race. The starter fired his gun and we were off. I settled into the middle of the group and then said to myself, "I can go faster than this," so I kicked it in and picked up my pace, passing some of the other runners. I looked up and saw only five guys ahead of me, picked up my pace again, and headed for the finish line. I was able to pass a couple of the runners and came in third place. Coach Crisco was so surprised that he came and gave me a big hug. I was the only one from our team who won a ribbon, third-place finish in the Southern West Virginia Track Meet.

There were only two weeks left of school, and on a beautiful day of blue skies and a bright sun, Pete Tolley, Jim Coulthard, and I had the last class free. We went outside to the nearby bridge and sat on the guardrail overlooking the river. Jim pulled a bag of Red Man Chewing Tobacco out of his pocket, put a big wad in his mouth, and offered Pete and me a chew. Jim and Pete chewed while they were playing baseball, but I had never chewed tobacco. So I was thinking, "Now is a good time to start." I took a big wad and put in my mouth. We sat there chewing and spitting in the river. We were enjoying the last few weeks of ninth grade and thinking about next year at Big Creek.

I was starting to get dizzy, so I spit out my tobacco, and we went to get on our bus to go home. Pete and Jim got off at their houses, and I continued on toward my house. I started yelling for the bus driver to stop the bus; I was getting sick. I had just gotten off the bus when I started throwing up, and the driver closed the door and drove away. I couldn't yell at him because I was busy throwing up. I had to walk the rest of the way home, and as I walked, I thought, "Don't think that I want to chew tobacco anymore." And I didn't.

When we moved down to Atwell, there were only my dad, Irene, Dennis, and me. The other four kids had graduated from high school and moved on with their lives. Walter was in the Air Force; Robert and Jerry were also in the Air Force and in Korea. Betty had moved to New Jersey where she was working in a glass factory. After the Korean War ended, Robert and Jerry enrolled at West Virginia University. They each had a car, but they didn't need both of the cars up at school so Jerry left his car at our house. None of us had a driver's license, but that didn't stop Dennis and me from driving the car all summer without our dad's permission or knowledge. We had to be on the lookout when we came to a railroad crossing in fear that our dad would be working nearby. Even though we had no car insurance or driver's license, we made it through the summer without getting pulled over by Hog Jaw. He was the police chief for the town of War.

It was a good summer, and I worked as a lifeguard at the Bartley swimming pool. Irene graduated from high school at the end of that year and married our next-door neighbor, Clinton Click. Clinton worked on the railroad with my dad and his dad. Irene and Clinton would later move to Michigan where my brother Walter and his wife had already relocated. Walter was discharged after his time was up in the Air Force. There was no work to be had in McDowell County, so Walt went to school in Chicago at DeVry, which is now a university. Then he moved to Michigan to work in the auto factory; when he retired he was the senior electrical engineer for a General Motors plant. It was later proven that wherever Walter went, the rest of the Evans kids would follow.

Dennis and I got to spend part of the summer with Walt and his family in Michigan. Back in those days, it was a long car ride from Atwell, West Virginia, to Inkster, Michigan, because there were no expressways. When we got out of the mountains in West Virginia, drove through Ohio, and then entered Michigan, Dennis and I couldn't believe how flat the ground was. It was all new to us because we had never been anywhere. We did spend a few weeks one summer at our aunt's house in Wise, Virginia. They had some smaller hills in that area, but it wasn't flat like Michigan. Dennis was older, and he was outside playing with the new kids he had met. I was just hanging around the house because Walt had a thing called a television, and we had never seen one of those. I watched as much as I could and even learned how to cook things besides pinto beans and fried potatoes. Walt also had a toaster, something we'd never had at home, and I knew nothing about a toaster. One morning I was fixing some toast and jelly for my breakfast, and I looked at the toaster and saw that my bread was stuck. I got a knife to free up the bread, and after a loud scream, the knife went flying up against the ceiling. I found out real fast what 110 volts of electricity can do to you. I have never done that trick again and don't plan on doing it again for the rest of my life.

We had a good time staying with Walt and his family that summer, but it was time to get back home and get ready for school. It would be my first year at Big Creek High School, and Dennis would graduate that year, 1955. I was excited but also fearful about playing football at Big Creek because I was still small and they had some big guys on the team. Then I thought about playing against the black kids. "The big kids at Big Creek can't be any tougher than those black kids," I told myself. "Lets go!"

Big Creek High School

RIDING ON THE bus for the first day of school in my sophomore year seemed like an eternity. It wasn't because it was a long distance to the school in War, but the roads were so crooked that it took a lot of time to get there. When I started at Big Creek, there were so many new kids because of all the junior high schools in the area. Kids from Coalwood, Berwind, Bartley, and War Junior High Schools made up the student body of Big Creek High School. McDowell County is the southernmost county in West Virginia, but the rest of the state knew about Big Creek because of our football team. In the three years that I played on the team, we had an impressive record of twenty-five wins, two losses, and two ties. Our offense scored 688 points, and the defense held the opposition to 130 points. So the rest of the state knew about our football program. We also won the county and all-area championships in the three years I was there. All of this was because of a lot of hard work and a great coaching staff. We had one of the best football coaches in the state, Coach Merrill Gainer.

Football practice started about two weeks before school

began, and we had to go through tackling drills, blocking drills, and sprints, and run the one-hundred-yard dash. Dave Rider was one of the fastest guys on our team and one of the hardest to tackle. In my first year of football, I got to dress for all the varsity games and played in the junior varsity games on Saturday afternoon. My only touchdown came in a game against Welch High School, and it was a two-yard run off the left tackle. I can't remember if I was tackled or just tripped over the goal line and fell into the end zone.

It was great because some of my family members were there. My brother Walt and his wife and my sister Irene and her husband, Clinton, were down from Michigan and got to see me play. My dad never came to any of my games because he didn't have a car, plus he didn't like the fact that I was playing. He said that I was going to get hurt because I was too small. I did get hurt during my sophomore year. I was playing on defense in practice one day and wasn't paying attention to what was going on. The next thing I knew I was lying on the ground with severe pain in my left knee. Mack Trout, an all-state fullback, had thrown a block on me and I didn't see him coming. Mack kept apologizing because he could see that I was in a lot of pain. It wasn't his fault; it was mine because I wasn't paying attention to what play they were running. I missed the next three weeks of the season, but I was able to come back and finish the rest of the season.

I had survived my first year of football at Big Creek. Now it was time for me to try out for the basketball team, and our coach was Merrill Gainer. Basketball wasn't his forte, but he was still a good coach. He didn't just teach us about our sports activities; he taught us about life and how to deal with other people. I was on the junior varsity team and Coach Gainer liked how I played on defense, so he brought me up to the varsity team to play against Welch. Don Marino was a guard and a very good shooter, and my assignment was to guard Marino. I had played against the black kids and they were good, so I knew that I could handle him. This dude from Welch was much better than I thought; he scored thirty-two points against me. After the game, during Coach Gainer's team meeting, he said that there was some doubt if this kid Marino was going to be an all-state player, but after this game he was certain to make all-state. When Monday came, I was back on the junior varsity team, but that didn't last long.

I had played junior high basketball at both War and Bartley Junior High Schools, so when they had their game against the players from the year before, I was invited to play at both schools. Coach Mams who was the Junior Varsity coach, didn't want me to play in both games, but I didn't listen to him and played in both games. When I came back to practice, Coach Mams showed me who was boss and cut me from the basketball team. My dad would be happy because I was no longer playing basketball, so I would be able to have his supper ready when he came home from work. Also, without basketball practice, I had more time to get to know some of the beautiful girls from Coalwood and Berwind. I already knew the ones from Bartley and War because I had attended both of those schools. My sophomore year was great.

My Junior Year

DURING THE SUMMER before my junior year at Big Creek, I got to go back and spend part of the summer in Michigan with my brother Walt and his family. My brother Jerry was also in Michigan working before he graduated from West Virginia University. Jerry and some of his friends invited me to play golf with them. I had never played but was willing to learn the game of golf. We played at the Huron Hills Golf Course in Ann Arbor, a course that I would play with all my brothers every Sunday years later when we were all living in Michigan. Also that summer Tom Turner, a Big Creek High School teammate of mine, was staying at his sister's house. She was married to one of my cousins, and they lived nearby. Tom and I had met some girls so we went on a double date. Those northern girls were having a hard time understanding the way Tom and I talked. That was okay because we would soon be back at Big Creek, starting our junior year, and those girls could understand us.

When football practice started, we had a very good group of players in the sophomore class. Among them were Gerald

Holbrook, Roger Bellamy, Kenny Fields, Gary Powell, Art Pruett, and Cecil Hampton, plus many more. We didn't lose a game that year but did have a tie that hurt our standing in the state rankings, and those in charge of the state rankings always said that we didn't play enough schools in West Virginia. We played a couple of schools that were in Virginia because they were located near us. One of those sophomore players was Fisheye (Cecil) Hampton, who played quarterback at War Junior High and was a good passer. After the third game of the season, Fisheye was inserted as the quarterback and Dave Rider was moved over to the running back position. Dave was a very good running back and would later play football at West Virginia University. I was playing defensive halfback and as a running back on offense. Dave Roberts and I also were used on punt returns and kickoff returns. Gerald Holbrook was another player from the sophomore class who played very well on the offensive and the defensive side of the ball. He was a tackle and played so well that he was selected to the all-county team.

My junior year on the football team was coming to an end, and I had played enough to earn my first varsity letter. Since I had been kicked off the basketball team the previous year by Coach Mams, I had a lot of free time until track season started. We didn't really have a track team that competed against other schools, but Coach Gainer made all of the football players come out for the track team. It was more like spring training for the upcoming football season that would start in the fall. Part of my free time was spent cooking supper for Dad and me. We were the only two left at home because Dennis had graduated and he and Clarence Blankenship joined the Air Force. I used to make a big pot of homemade chili for us. We would eat that chili about four days in a row because all I had to do was heat it up for three of those meals. After I left home, I don't think my dad ever ate another bowl of chili. Going back to where I said, "All I had to do was heat it up," it was not like today where I could just stick it in the microwave. I had to build a fire in the old wood-burning cookstove and then heat it up.

That wasn't the only thing that was heating up. Our next-door neighbors had three daughters; the oldest one was two years younger than me, and the next one was about 3½ years younger. The oldest one rode the school bus home with me, and when I start fixing supper, she would sneak over to my house. We would start talking, and the next thing I knew, we were kissing. It was always about this time that her mother would yell, "Betty, get out of that house and get back home." Sometimes I thought her mother was standing on a box and peeking in the window.

One time her mother's timing was off. We were kissing and I had just gotten the top hook of her bra undone when there came that yell, "Betty, get out of that house." Before she could finish her yell, I had the top hook back on the bra. Then the younger sister also started sneaking into the house while I was cooking. Their mother was like a mother duck watching over her babies. I was going to have to come up with a better plan or just give up. These neighbors were really great friends. The mother was the hardest-working woman I ever knew. The father was a coal miner and had broken his back while working in the mines, so he was limited to how much work he could do. I saw the mother put a new roof on their house. She also plowed up a big garden area and did all of the hoeing in the garden. And that was in addition to all of the things a woman had to do back in those days, such as cooking, housecleaning, washing clothes, ironing, and making sure that her daughters didn't sneak into my house.

It was about this time in my junior year that Dad and I got our first phone. I can still remember the number; it was two shorts and a long. We were on a party line with eight other people. When you received a phone call, you could hear some of the neighbors picking up their phones to listen in. So when you were talking on the phone with your girlfriend, you had to watch what you said. Not only did we get our first phone but we also got our first television. You could only get about three channels, and they were fuzzy; because of the mountains the reception was poor. The TV channels came on at 6:00 a.m. and started the day with the playing of "The Star-Spangled Banner."

That same year one of my buddies, Roger Gates, said to me, "I am going over to Welch tomorrow to get my driver's license. Do you want to go with me?" I had learned how to drive when I was twelve years old, and the summer before, Dennis and I had driven our brother's car so I was ready for my license. (Something to point out about the test we had to take for our driver's license. Back in those days, cars didn't have turn signals; you had to use your hand to signal which direction you were turning.) Roger and I both passed our test, so he got to drive his dad's car, but my dad didn't own a car. What was I going to drive?

I went home that evening and told my dad that I had gotten my driver's license. He wanted to know what I was going to do with it. Well, I guess I could use it as an ID card. We went to church on Sunday as we had done for the last sixteen years of my life. One of Dad's friends at church was a car salesman working in Welch, so my dad talked with him about buying a used car. He sold my dad a 1951 Ford. I had to go with my dad to get the car because my dad had never owned or driven a car (he was fifty-five years old at the time). We picked up the car on a Saturday morning, and as soon as we got back home, Dad wanted me to teach him how to drive. My job was a bit harder because they only made cars with a manual transmission and my dad was having a hard time getting the clutch and the gas petal to work together for a smooth takeoff. He was also forgetting to use the clutch in conjunction with the brake when coming to a stop. After a couple of weeks of practice, he was improving enough to try to pass his driver's test, and that he did. So get all the kids and women off the roads because George Evans had his driver's license! I have often wondered how many kids taught their dads how to drive.

I was still doing most of the driving and every Saturday drove up to Deskin's Super Market in English to buy our groceries for the week. I had to get the items to make another big pot of homemade chili. Dad drove us to church on Sunday mornings. During my junior year of high school, these three things—the phone, the TV, and the car that Dad bought for us—were the reason why all my siblings said that I was spoiled. That wasn't true because I got more whippings than any of them. I wasn't spoiled; I was hardheaded.

I got to use the car for dates on Saturday nights and even learned how to park. We used to park up on a mountaintop so we could get a radio station out of Del Rio, Texas, and listen to Wolfman Jack. He was one of the hottest DJs at that time. Wolfman Jack was always selling something on the radio, and there were rumors that he was selling autographed pictures of Jesus.

Since we had moved down to Atwell, Roger Bellamy and I had become best friends, He lived just across the river and around the big curve from my house. I spent most of my time at his house because it was too lonely staying home alone while my dad was at work. Roger and I would drive down to Bradshaw on the weekend because we knew lots of girls down there. They went to Iaeger High School, and we were near the end of the boundaries for the Big Creek school district. We were very good friends even though they went to one of our rival schools for football and basketball.

My junior year in high school saw a lot of changes in my life. I went from walking or hitchhiking to driving our car to get where I needed to go. One Saturday night I drove over to Roger Bellamy's house; we were going down to Bradshaw for the evening. When I stopped to pick him up, he came down the hill with his black pegged pants on but was not wearing a shirt. He had his pink shirt in his hands. I asked him if this was the new style, and he told me that he had to sew a button on his shirt. He had a needle and thread, and after completing the job, he stuck the needle with some thread still hanging from it in the sun visor in front of me. The next morning when my dad was driving to church without me, I guess the thread was swinging in front of him like a pendulum. As he tried to get the thread wrapped around the needle, he forgot about driving, ran off the road, and totaled the car. He even received a few stitches in his forehead. He must have thought that he was in the rail car they used for going to their job each morning. You didn't have to steer it; all you had to do was push a lever forward to go forward and pull it back to go in reverse. After he got his stitches removed, he went back to

Welch and bought a 1953 Chevrolet. Just like the Jeffersons, we were moving on up.

Dad was starting to complain about having chili too often, so I went back to our old menu of pinto beans, fried potatoes, and cornbread with some green onions and iced tea. I had to keep him happy because I needed the car more often. The church that Dad and I went to sat on the side of a hill in Raysal. Gerald Holbrook's dad and my dad were the two men in charge of the church, so they decided that we needed to dig out from under the church and build a basement. During the summer between my junior and senior year, Gerald and I were responsible for digging out for the basement. That was our way of staying in shape for the upcoming football season, but I want you to know that neither Gerald nor I volunteered for this job. We did have some help from other members of the church, and the job was completed before school started.

My Senior Year

ON THE FIRST day of school, our principal, Mr. Turner, had all of the students assembled in the auditorium for his welcoming message. He also was welcoming the new sophomore class and said if they needed any help finding the way to their classrooms, the seniors would help direct them to their next class. So being good seniors, anytime a sophomore asked us for directions to a certain classroom, we would point them in the opposite direction. That way they would learn much quicker.

The school year didn't get started without some delays. A small group of black students from Excelsior High School came to enroll at Big Creek, and back in those days, the schools were segregated in our state. Mr. Turner didn't allow them to enroll the first day they arrived. Part of the student body wasn't happy with the black kids trying to enroll, so they went outside and sat in the bleachers. I wasn't one of them because I knew lots of the black kids from Excelsior. We had played football, basketball, and baseball with some of them, and Buddy Pennington ate at my house just about every Sunday. My dad had always taught us that we were no better than anyone else and we were all

God's children. After the second day of the protest, with some of the football players among them, Coach Gainer went out to the bleachers and told the football players that if they didn't get back to their classrooms, they could turn in their uniforms and clean out their lockers. The football players got up and went back to their class as did some of the other protesters because Coach Gainer was respected by the entire student body.

The number of black kids was getting smaller each day as was the number of protesters. Mr. Turner was caught off guard and didn't know how to handle the situation so he called for advice from the superintendent of McDowell County schools. The black students went back to Excelsior High School, and integration would happen a few years later. This is how my senior year in high school started, and I think that living through that experience has made me a better person.

In my senior year we had 758 students at Big Creek High School, and there were 225 seniors. We were led by Pete Tolley as president, Tom Turner as vice president, Linda Harlow as secretary, and Jim Coulthard as treasurer, a good group of leaders. I think that our graduating class was the largest class to graduate from Big Creek High School.

Football practice had begun three weeks before school started. When we started practice, I had gained some weight and now weighed in at 142 pounds and stood five feet eight inches of solid muscle. Still on the small side, I played with a lot of injuries. Coach Gainer used to call me "Luke" because he said that I was like Luke Appling, whose nickname was "Old Aches and Pains." Appling was a shortstop for the Chicago White Sox baseball team. I was still playing a defensive halfback, and I had been moved to a split-end position. Some of my injuries were caused by Coach Gainer. The previous year we were running plays against the first team defense; Ralph Crandle was a defensive end, and I was a running back. Ralph was about six foot three and weighed about 195 pounds; and I was five foot seven and 125 pounds. I was running around the tight end and made a big gain on the play. Coach Gainer got mad at Ralph and chewed him out for letting a little guy like me get by him. Coach Gainer yelled to Coach Mams and said, "Run the same play." I thought, "Thanks a lot, Coach. You've got Ralph mad and now he is going to kill me." So we ran the same play, and there waiting for me was a pissed-off Ralph. He picked me up and slammed me to the ground, and I landed on my elbow. My elbow was full of water and swollen for the rest of the season. I think Coach Gainer liked me because I did play with injuries and I wasn't afraid to make tackles on defense; plus he needed some one to kid and pick on during practice.

Our three weeks of practice were over, school had started, and we were ready for our first football game. Pineville was our challenger for the season opener, and we had beaten them for the last eight years. Dave Roberts took the opening kickoff, ran toward me, and handed me the ball. I was able to get about forty yards before I was tackled. It was a good start, and we didn't have much trouble handling the Pineville Minutemen. We won the game 21–0, and now we were preparing for our second game, which was against Norfolk-Elkhorn. We rolled over them with no problems and won the game 24–0. This was our second shutout, and our defense had not been scored on. We were led by Danny Thacker as linebacker, and Gerald Holbrook and Pete Tolley also were standouts on the defensive team. Fisheye was an outstanding quarterback, and we had Art

Pruett at running back, so we had no problems when we went up against Tazwell, beating them 27–6 for our third win of the season.

Next on our schedule was Welch, the largest town in McDowell County. We looked at their players as city kids, but they also had more kids to choose from to field their football team. They could be a good team, but we were able to get a 19–6 victory and stay undefeated. Our next game was with the Gary Coaldiggers, and they were always a rough team. They had a kid from Poland who was in his second year of playing football. He was one of the hardest-running fullbacks I ever tackled. When I was able to tackle him, he would say in his broken English, "OK, you," and I would say in my hillbilly English, "Hell no, I am not OK. You just about killed me." He would laugh and go back to the huddle to get ready to do it again. Because I had so many good players around me, we were able to hang on and beat Gary 27–18, five wins in a row.

We would be traveling to Princeton for our next game, and I would be playing against one of my cousins, Jim Evans; he was a tackle on the offensive line. During our pregame warm-ups, Fisheye was going through his passing patterns. I was going deep, and Fisheye led me with a high arching pass that I was able to leap for and make with a one-handed catch. I could hear a roar from the crowd, and it made chills go down my spine. I wished I could have done it during the game. Even without my crowd-pleasing catch, though, we were able to hang on and beat Princeton 14–7, our toughest game thus far. The next week we would be playing a team we had never played before, Oak Hill.

The only thing I knew about Oak Hill was that was where

country singer Hank Williams had died a few years earlier. Oak Hill was always high in the state ranking at the end of the year, and we would soon find out why. On the kickoff, Oak Hill received the ball and it was fielded by a black kid—and he was fast. I was on the kickoff team and the first one down the field. Back in those days, our football helmets did not have a face mask mounted on them. I hit the runner low and his foot smashed into my nose, breaking it and cutting me across the bridge of my nose. When I came off the field bleeding, Coach Ganier looked at me with a big grin on his face and said, "Good tackle, Luke." Things went downhill from there. Our offense couldn't get any type of ground game going against their defense. We ended up losing our first game of the year 12–0 to Oak Hill. I don't know if it was because we lost, but after the game I felt like I had been run over by a Mack Truck. There was no time to sit around and feel sorry for ourselves because Bluefield was next on our schedule, and that team was always hard to beat.

On Tuesday, about halfway through practice, Coach Gainer blew the whistle and called the team around him. He said, "Don't look up on the hillside," and about half of the players looked up at the hillside. Coach said he thought some-one was up there with binoculars, spying on our practice. He instructed Coach Mams to go inside and call the police and have them check it out. We stayed in a huddle around Coach Gainer for a few more minutes, and then we started running some simple plays so as not to give away any of our game plans. Then we noticed that the police had arrived on the hillside, and after talking to the stranger for a few minutes, they left. Before our practice was over the policeman came and talked to Coach

Gainer. The stranger was a former Big Creek football player who had played college football and was now assistant football coach at Bluefield. He knew the area and knew a good spot where he could spy on our practice and try to get our game plan. All of this was reported to the Welch newspaper, and it was reported for the next couple of days on the radio and in the newspaper.

On Friday night we were playing in their stadium, which was much larger than ours. I think because of all the publicity about this matchup, we had eleven thousand fans attend this game. I believe that was a state record for the number of people attending a high school football game. It was a tough game, and we were leading 19–18 late in the fourth quarter. They were moving the ball down the field and had the ball on our 40-yard line with just a little over a minute to play. Their quarterback dropped back to pass and their tight end had gotten behind me, but Gerald and Danny were putting pressure on the quarterback. Therefore, he wasn't able to get as much on the pass, and I was able to make up some ground and knock the ball down. That was their fourth down, so we got the ball back with about forty-eight seconds left in the game. As I was running to knock down the pass, the mistake I made against Bartley when I was in the ninth grade flashed through my mind, but this time the results were different. I was never a star football player, but that was my greatest moment, which I can still remember. We won the game 19–18 and in front of the largest crowd we had ever played before.

Our next scheduled game was at Man High School; it was a smaller school and had never beaten us in football. Man High School was located near the town of Logan, West Virginia, and it was a long bus ride up there. We had no problem in getting a 32–0 win over them, bringing our record to eight wins and one loss, with one game remaining on our schedule.

The cheerleaders always led a pep rally after lunch on Fridays before the game that night. The cheerleaders would ask different football players to give a pep talk to the other students, and I always refused to talk because I was very shy. Danny Thacker and Pete Tolley were our captains, and they did most of the talking. We attended our last pep rally of the season, and then we were loaded on a school bus for a long ride to Virginia to play Richlands. It was always hard to get any information about their football program because our local newspaper didn't report much about the schools in Virginia. The only information we had was what Coach Marron would get while scouting their game the week before we played them. He had collected enough information about their team, and we had an easy time beating them 20–0 in our last game of the 1956 football season.

For me, it was sad to end our season. I had been playing football for the last six years of school and I'd had two great coaches, Gainer and Payne. They had taught me a lot about life and why teamwork was so important in anything you try to accomplish in life. I would also miss football because some of the pretty girls in school gravitated to the basketball players, and I no longer played basketball since Coach Mams had me kicked off the team. I was proud of our football team and the record we had compiled in my three years at Big Creek High School. We won twenty-five games, lost two, and tied two, and the last West Virginia school to beat us was Oak Hill in 1951. Big Creek High School was always known for its football program, especially since Coach Gainer had been in charge. In my senior year, five of our players wereselected to the all-county team: Danny Thacker, Pete Tolley, Dave Roberts, Dave Farmer, and Gerald Holbrook. Making the all-area team were Danny Thacker, Pete Tolley, and Gerald Holbrook, and making the all-state team was Danny Thacker. Pete Tolley would play football at West Virginia University for four years. Danny Thacker had many scholarship offers to play football in college but turned them down to pursue an engineering degree. As an adult I have had lots of problems with my knees, and I am sure that some of those problems are a result of playing football when I was younger. I wouldn't trade the experience of playing football for Big Creek High School with all of my former teammates for any pain relief. No pain, no gain.

Now that football season was over and neither Roger Bellamy, Gerald Holbrook, Kenny Fields, nor I played basketball at Big Creek, we had more time to hang out in Bradshaw. Some of the local boys didn't like us hanging out in their town and talking to their girls. We had some problems but none that Gerald and Roger couldn't take care of as Kenny and I sat back and watched. We were lovers, not fighters. We spent most of our time at Roger Bellamy's girlfriend's house. Her mother, Mrs. Wolf, was such a nice lady, and she always made us feel welcome in her home. She looked forward to having us come every weekend. She baked a cake or some cookies for us to eat, and I have never seen a football player turn down food, especially sweets. We also spent time in the Bradshaw Café. There was a jukebox in the corner, and the girls were always playing Elvis Presley songs. Most of the guys didn't like Elvis because the girls went crazy over him. Years later, I must admit that I too liked to listen to some of his songs. We used to listen to "Blue Christmas" as our kids decorated our Christmas tree.

My dad was letting me use the car more often so I would pick up Roger Bellamy and the other guys. We'd spend Saturday night in Bradshaw and sometimes go to the movies on Sunday after church service was over. At that time, Roger was the only one of us who had a steady girlfriend, but Kenny, Gerald, and I had good friends who were girls, and we did our fair share of kissing in the movie theater. I couldn't tell you the name of any movies we saw, but we enjoyed our time with the beautiful girls of Bradshaw. I was a year older than Roger, Kenny, and Gerald, and I heard that all three of them had steady girlfriends in Bradshaw while I was in the Air Force.

Roger Bellamy had two pretty sisters, and one of them was four years younger than me; I kinda had a crush on her. One day I went over to visit and she was lying on her bed and crying. I went in and held her hand, and I asked why she was crying. She said that she had a toothache and it hurt, so I gently gave her a kiss. She quit crying and said it didn't hurt anymore. At that point in my life, I thought I should become a dentist, but after further thought I wondered what I would do if some of my patients were men. No, that wouldn't work. So my dental career was over before it started.

Roger and his family became a big part of my life; his mother treated me like I was one of her own kids. The Bellamy family had replaced the Blankenship family who lived next door to us when we were in Excelsior. When we moved to Atwell, the mountains were much steeper than the ones near our house in Excelsior, so Roger and our other friends didn't spend as much time roaming the hills like we did in Excelsior. Plus, we had a good baseball field just down the river from our house, where we spent many hours playing ball. Located at the Atwell ballpark was a monument dedicated to ninety-one miners who had been killed in an explosion at the number one mine in Bartley in January 1940. Some of the kids I went to school with had lost their dads in that mine explosion. Roger's dad was a coal miner, but he worked in another mine. The coal mines were slowing down, and some of the people had to find work in other states. Roger's dad was one of those miners who relocated to Cleveland, Ohio, for a job.

Roger's older brother, Bob, had served in the army after graduating from Big Creek High School and ended up with a job in Cleveland, Ohio; that's also why Roger's dad went to work there. Roger still had one more year of high school at that time, and he wanted to finish at Big Creek, where he was one of the star football players. Roger, his mother, and two sisters stayed in Atwell while he finished high school. After an undefeated football season, Roger and Gerald Holbrook both earned scholarships to play football at Virginia Polytechnic Institute (VPI), which is now Virginia Tech. Roger played one year and then moved up to Cleveland, Ohio, to be with his family and start his career as a tool and die maker. Gerald went on to play four years at VPI. Kenny Fields was also a star on the undefeated 1957 football team at Big Creek High School, but Kenny also was good at baseball and played baseball at Lincoln Memorial University in Harrogate, Tennessee. The Bradshaw gang had gone their separate ways, but I am sure that we all have fond memories of those beautiful girls and the good times we had with them as we were growing up in McDowell County, West Virginia.

Meanwhile, back at Big Creek High School to finish out my senior year, I was a member of the Key Club and we were going on a trip to West Virginia University for the weekend. One of my brothers was still going to school there, and it would be a chance to see him. Tom Todd's dad let us use his '98 Oldsmobile for the trip, and I did one of the stupidest things in my life. There were five guys in our car, and we were trading off on the driving. When it was my time to drive, I asked Tom how fast the car would go. We were on a long stretch of straightaway road, which was rare in West Virginia. Tom said, "Let's see how fast it will go." Well, I opened it up and it was up to 105 miles per hour. Back then I didn't think anything about it, but now I think of the many things that could have gone wrong, such as blowing a tire, losing control, or being stopped by a state trooper. Sometimes I think that I must have had an angel riding on my shoulder for all the stupid things I did as a teenager. I am glad that nothing happened to Mr. Todd's car on that trip to West Virginia University.

Springtime in the mountains of McDowell County was beautiful with all of the dogwood and redbud trees. These trees added so much color to the mountains, along with the wildflowers that had started to bloom. Spring also meant that it was time for our senior prom. Who was I going to ask? I had dated a few girls from Coalwood, and there was one whom I wanted to ask to the prom, but I was afraid that she would say no. So I asked one of my buddies from Coalwood to talk to her to see if she even knew who I was, and she did. She was a tall, beautiful girl and a very smart girl, and that is why I didn't think she would say yes if I got up the nerve to ask her to the prom. I would talk to her as we passed in the hallway, and then we started sitting together in the auditorium before class each morning. I asked her to go to the prom with me, and she said yes. When the guys from Coalwood found out that she was going to the prom with me, they started kidding me that I had to be approved by her parents.

Later that week she asked me to come over to her house on Saturday night to meet her parents. After all, this would be her first date; she was a sophomore and more into books than boys. So I cleaned up and wore my best clothes when I went to meet her parents. They were southern folks from Biloxi, Mississippi, and were very nice. I guess I did okay because on Monday when I saw Eleanor, she told me that we were going to the prom. On prom night I got dressed in my only suit, and I had bought Eleanor a corsage to wear. She had large breasts so I wasn't going to pin it on her in front of her parents. I asked if her mother would do it for me. On the car ride to the dance, I asked Eleanor if her mother had given her any advice, and she said that her mother told her not to let me French-kiss her. How did her mother know what I wanted to do? We had a good time dancing, and then as we sat in the car in the parking lot, I taught her how to French kiss. I got to go over to her house a few more times to see her before the school year ended. Then I kept in contact with her by letters when I was in the Air Force. I never forgot what a great time we had at my senior prom and on her first date. Thanks, Eleanor, for the memories.

End of My Senior Year

DURING THE LAST two years of high school, it was just me and my dad living at home. It was lonely for me, not having anyone I could talk with; that is why I spent most of my free time over at Roger Bellamy's house. Dad would get up each morning, start the fire in our wood-burning cookstove, and make biscuits and gravy for the two of us. He only knew how to make breakfast for seven kids and now he was cooking the same amount for just him and me. He went to work, and I did the dishes and cleaned up before I went to school. Now that I wasn't playing any sports, it was my responsibility to cook our supper. After we ate, my dad sat down to read his newspaper as I washed the dishes. Then I was off to Roger's house until it was dark, and when it gets dark down in the hills of West Virginia, it really gets dark; there were no streetlights or any other kind of lights near our home. One night I left Roger's house and it was so dark that I had to get down on my knees and feel around to find the bridge. I was able to stumble over to a gate going into our yard. As I was extending out my hand to find the gate, I put my hand on something that had fur on it and it let out big moo and started moving; it was a cow standing there sleeping. The next morning there were two piles on the ground, one was human and one was bovine. I don't know who was scared the most, me or the cow.

Not only did I do the cooking for our supper and wash the dishes but I also had to do the laundry. That was a big job because we didn't have running water in our house. I had to carry water from a stream running off the side of a cliff up in Atwell holler; a lot of folks got their water from the same stream. All we had was an old Maytag washing machine, and I had to hang the clothes on a clothesline in our yard to dry. On the weekends I would sweep the entire house and mop the kitchen floor. I also went shopping at Deskin's Market for our groceries for the week. All of my siblings say that I was spoiled. Now I ask you, does that sound like I was spoiled?

The Big Flood

JUST BEFORE MY senior year ended, we had lots of rain that caused the worst flood in my lifetime. It washed away the big bridge at Atwell. We were lucky that our car was on the other side of the river when the bridge washed away, but how were we going to get across the river? After the river went down, my dad and some of the neighbors rigged up a pulley system with a boat attached to it so we could cross the river. If the boat wasn't on your side of the river, all you had to do was pull it over to your side and you would be able to cross. My brother Robert had come home from West Virginia University for the weekend, and his car was parked by the road. I needed to go shopping for our groceries, so I asked Roger Bellamy if he wanted to go with me, and he said yes. Robert had spent four years in the Air Force and was in the Korean War, so he was older than most kids he was going to school with at West Virginia University. Robert had lots of girlfriends, and sometimes he had been caught with other guys' girlfriends. This happened one night up at the Toot and Tell beer joint. Robert was with another guy's girlfriend in the back seat of his car, and the guy found out about it and started shooting at Robert's car. He put a bullet hole in the back door, but Robert was able to get away. So while Robert was sleeping after his long drive home, I got his car keys, and Roger and I went shopping in his car. When we got back home with all of the groceries, we didn't want to use the boat to get all of the groceries across the river. About that time my neighbor drove his pickup truck across the river, so I told Roger that we should try doing it too. Roger didn't think that it was a good idea, but I started into the water and got about half way across and the motor died. I looked into the backseat of the car and saw water pouring through the bullet hole in the door. I had some of the groceries sitting on the floor, so I had to crawl into the backseat and get them up off the floor. My neighbor saw what I had done, and he used his bulldozer to pull us out of the river. Robert wasn't real happy when he found out what I had done to his car. That darn old bullet hole.

Off into the Wild Blue Yonder

MY SENIOR YEAR was winding down and I didn't know if I was supposed to be happy or sad. I think I was a little on the sad side because school was a social thing for me and now I would be leaving it behind; all the friends I had grown up with would be out of my life. I also was sad because I knew that my dad couldn't afford to send me to college and all my friends would be going off to college. Just as my four brothers before me graduated from Big Creek High School and joined the US Air Force, I followed in their footsteps. My graduation was held on May 23, 1957, and my dad was there to watch his baby boy get his high school diploma. My dad and I never talked about what I would do after graduation, but I think he may have known what I was going to do. Now he would have no one living with him and no one to fix his supper when he got home from work. I think back about my dad and how he was able to raise seven kids without the love and support of his wife. How nice it would be at the end of a hard day at work to come home to a wife who had fixed a good supper, and then go to bed and be able to hold your wife in your arms and drift off to sleep. He never had that for nineteen years while we were growing up. Now I was getting ready to join the US Air Force, and he would be completely alone.

Everything happened so fast after graduation. I went to Welch to talk with the Air Force recruiter and take a test. He told me that I would be leaving in about two weeks and he would give me a call. When I got home that afternoon, the recruiter called and said that a bus was leaving that day and a couple of my friends were leaving also. He asked if I would like to go right away. I told him that I would be there in time to leave. I had to write a quick note to my dad to let him know what I was doing. I got over to Welch and met my two friends who were leaving with me, Tommy Richardson from Big Creek and Larry Miller from Iaeger; I got to know Larry because he lived in Bradshaw. We rode the bus to Beckley, where we were sworn in to the United States Air Force for the next four years.

Basic Training

ON THE BUS ride from Welch to Beckley, Larry, Tommy, and I talked about how nice the Air Force recruiter had been to us. When we arrived in Beckley to be sworn in, everyone was still nice to all of us new recruits. There were about forty guys and a couple of girls waiting to be sworn in. The sergeant in charge asked if anyone wanted to change his or her mind; no one stepped forward. Once we were sworn in, the voice and attitude of the sergeant changed; it was like the difference between night and day. He had us fall in line, and we marched out to a bus for a trip to Charleston, West Virginia, where we boarded a plane at the airport. This was the first time I had ever flown on a plane. I got a seat next to a window so I could see places that I had never been before. Our first stop was Nashville, Tennessee, and then we continued to our final destination, which was Lackland Air Force Base in San Antonio, Texas. On May 23rd I was in War, West Virginia, and on May 27th I was in San Antonio, Texas, for twelve weeks of basic training. Everything was happening so fast.

After we got off of the plane, we were shipped by bus to the base and were assigned to a barracks and then a bed. I didn't get a lot of sleep the first night because I was thinking about my dad and the fact that I didn't get to talk to him before I left. Also there were some guys crying because this was the first time they had ever been away from home and they missed their mothers. We were not issued uniforms until the fourth day that we were there. We were lined up to march over to the mess hall for lunch, and another flight of airmen that had been there long enough to get their uniforms called us "rainbows" because we were dressed in so many colors. When I went into the Air Force, I was five foot seven and weighed 128 pounds, with a twenty-eight-inch waistline. I had lost some weight since football season because I was at 142 pounds when the season started. We were issued new uniforms, and I threw away the old clothes that I had worn for the last five days because we hadn't brought a change of clothes with us. Now I was feeling like I was in the Air Force. I was also feeling like a sheep after getting its hair sheared off; we didn't need a comb.

Get That Airman a
New Set of Uniforms

IN THE AIR Force, basic training is simple; we were not trained to fight in combat but trained more in the technical field. Football practice at Big Creek High School was much harder than my basic training at Lackland Air Force Base. After two weeks of training, our flight was divided into two groups for some track and field events. One guy from each group was selected to be the captain, and because of Tommy and Larry, I was selected as captain of our group. Each group had a TI, or training instructor, assigned to the group. I think that the TIs had a side bet between them that the loser had to buy beer for the winning TI. My TI came over to me and said, "If you don't win, your ass is grass and I am the mower." Nothing like putting pressure on me, but somehow my group won the competition, no thanks to me. We had competition in the one hundred-yard dash, the fifty-yard dash, push-ups, chin-ups, half-mile run, and climbing over a high wall using a rope to assist you. The losing captain in the other group was a big guy, about six foot four and 210 pounds, and for the rest of our basic training he was always looking for a chance to kick my butt. It never happened.

We were all given a general aptitude test that took four hours to complete, and how well we did on the test determined how long we were going to be at Lackland for basic training. My highest score was in electronics, and I was asked what type of training I would like to do. My brother Jerry was a radar operator during the Korean War, so I told them I wanted to be a radar operator. I was selected to go to tech school in Biloxi, Mississippi, and would only be spending four weeks at Lackland.

One morning after we had been marching, we were standing at attention, waiting for an inspection from our captain. We were dressed in our class A uniforms, and the captain walked down each line checking out each airman. When he came to me, he stood in front of me longer than he had at most of the other airmen. Then he walked on down the line about three airmen past me and came back in front of me and asked, "Airman, how much weight have you gained?" I said, "Sir, I don't know." The captain turned to the first sergeant and said, "Get this airman a new set of uniforms." I guess because I was eating three meals a day, going to bed early every night, and not out chasing girls, I had put on some extra weight. So long to my twenty-eight-inch waistline. I wish that I could say it was my bulging muscles that were popping off my buttons, but not so. I was issued a complete set of uniforms before I was transferred to Biloxi for my tech school training. All of the time that I was at Lackland AFB, we were never given a pass to go off base, so we never saw any girls in town. Once in a while, though, we would see a flight of girls who were in basic training. We didn't get too excited because they were putting something in our food or milk that would prevent that from happening.

We were transported by bus from Lackland AFB to Keesler AFB for tech school training. When we got to the New Orleans area, we were scheduled to stop at a restaurant but because a hurricane had just passed through the area, there was no power. We were unable to get our lunch, so we drove on to Biloxi and got there about 8:00 p.m. I can still remember what a big difference this place was from where we had been. In Texas it was very hot, and it was hot in Biloxi. too, but there was a breeze blowing off the Gulf of Mexico that made it so much more pleasant. The atmosphere on base was much more relaxed than what we had in Texas. I would be in school for six hours a day and then have two hours for extended basic training to complete my required twelve weeks. Most of the basic training was marching out to an area where several B-24 bombers were sitting. Keesler AFB was used for all types of electronics training and pilot training. Many of the pilots were from the Middle East and they all had beards, something we couldn't do in the US Air Force. The best part about being in Biloxi was that on the weekends we could request an off-base pass to go into town. That is where I learned how to drink beer and throw up without getting it on my military shoes.

A Radar Operator

BEING A RADAR operator involved learning three different positions to complete a mission. First you sat in the dark with a radar monitor to learn how to detect any aircraft flying within a 250-mile radius of your location. Once you identified a flying object, you called your plotter by headphone. The plotter was a guy sitting behind a large Plexiglas map of the surrounding area where you were located. He would take the information you called in to him and plot the location of the IP (initial plot) on the big map. He had to write the information backward so the coordinator could read it and pass it on to the control tower. The IP was followed and the aircraft's position was plotted about every two minutes. With this information you could determine the speed of the plane and the altitude; sometimes you also could determine the type of plane by the size of the blip on the radar screen. The control tower took the information that you gave them and identified the aircraft. You continued to track an aircraft until it was off your radar screen. The big Plexiglas map was laid out in grid coordinates so you always knew where the plane was flying. We had to learn each position, and we rotated positions every two hours. If we had been out drinking before coming to work, it was hard to stay awake while sitting in front of a radar monitor watching the cursor go around. If we fell asleep, though, we could be court-martialed.

While I was stationed in Biloxi, a couple of my buddies and I had a weekend pass, so we decided to go over to the beach in Gulfport, Mississippi. We were swimming, drinking beer, and lying on the beach, trying to attract some girls. We did more swimming and drinking than we did attracting pretty girls. I did manage to get the worst sunburn I'd ever had in my life, and I ended up in the base hospital for severe burns. My first sergeant said that I could be court-martialed for destroying government property. It sounded like the coal miners who sold their soul to the company store.

The Big Lie

MY RADAR OPERATOR'S class was just about over and I would be shipped out to another Air Force base once I had completed the class. We were all asked to fill out a form with our first, second, and third base of choice where we would like to be stationed. We were told that they would try to give us our first base of choice. My first choice was Germany, my second was Japan, and my third was Michigan. The following week a list was posted announcing where everyone would be stationed. When I was able to push my way close enough to read the assignments, I saw "Roger Evans—Tin City, Alaska." So much for the big lie. Some of the guys were happy with their assignments; they were going to Germany, Florida, and California. But I was going to a remote site in Alaska. Some of our instructors had been stationed on different bases before they became instructors, and one of them told me, "You will like it up there; you will have a woman behind every tree." The only problem was that there wasn't a tree within a thousand miles of where I was going to be for the next year.

Tin City, Alaska, was thirty-five miles south of the Artic

Circle and ninety miles northwest of Nome, Alaska. The closest place to us was Russia; it was only seventeen miles away. Our radar site at Tin City was part of the DEW (detection and early warning) line, and the Air Force had lots of remote sites around the coast of Alaska to detect any aircraft coming from Russia. My brother Robert had been stationed at Point Barrow, Alaska, before he was shipped to Korea during the war. So if he could do it, I could do it too. Only two more weeks of school and there would be thirty new radar operators graduating from the 710 AC&W (Aircraft Control & Warning) class and shipped out to save the world.

I had a thirty-day leave before I would be flown up to Alaska. So I went back home to see my dad and let him know that I was sorry for leaving without talking to him. He was glad to see me and proud that I had followed in my brothers' footsteps. I had been gone for only four months, but I was surprised to see how much smarter my dad had gotten since I left home. After leaving his house, I went to Michigan to see part of my family before flying to Seattle, Washington.

North to Alaska

I FLEW OUT to McCord Air Force Base in Tacoma, Washington, and I had to stay there until they were able to get me a flight up to Anchorage, Alaska. It was so beautiful in that part of our country; it looked like you could walk right over to Mount Rainier, but it was fifty miles away. I lived in the mountains back in West Virginia, but they weren't so high that you had snow on them year round. I loved the West Virginia mountains, but it was great to see other parts of the United States. After we landed in Anchorage, we transferred to another plane that flew us into Fairbanks, Alaska. I spent the next two weeks there because I had to get a checkup from a doctor and have some dental work done before I was flown out to my remote radar site. Just before we got to Fairbanks, our pilot told us to look out the windows on the left side of the plane. It looked as if I could reach out and touch Mount McKinley, so majestic, the highest point in North America. I had only been in the Air Force four months, and already I had seen so much and got the chance to fly in planes; what a change for a country boy.

From Fairbanks to Nome I was on a lot of small planes. We had to land at Galena because of problems with the plane, so I had to sleep in the building where they were working on the plane. The next day the plane was fixed and we were on our way to Nome. At one time, during the Gold Rush days, the population of Nome was over two hundred thousand people, but now the town only had about four thousand people living there. When we landed in Nome, the weather was getting bad, and we couldn't fly in the small plane that was going to take me the last ninety miles to my remote site. The plane also was used to deliver the mail to our remote site, and sometimes we would go for weeks before the mail plane could deliver because of the bad weather. We finally had some clear skies and were off with a load of mail to my remote site, and I reached my final destination. The plane that flew me in had to take back four dead men who had spent their year at the remote site. When they were leaving, their plane was caught in a downdraft and crashed into the Bering Sea, and the men were killed.

Welcome to
Tin City, Alaska

AS WE WERE flying to my final destination, I was looking out the window of the plane for the trees that were supposed to have a woman behind each one of them. There were none to be found, just frozen, snow-covered tundra for miles around. I reported to the base commander and was given a tour of the radar site. All of the buildings were connected with covered hallways in between each building because of the severe cold weather in the winter. On the tour I was taken to the "melter," where we would shovel snow into an open pit so the snow could be melted and provide us with water in the winter. The snow was heated in a holding tank and then the liquid ran downhill into another holding tank located inside of our heated building. It was hard to melt enough snow to provide water for the needs of 110 men, so we were limited to one shower per week during the winter. Everyone had to spend an eight-hour shift shoveling snow into the melter, and this was done seven days a week for the entire winter.

I was taken to the place where I would be working; it was a locked building and I had to have a security clearance to enter the workplace. We had three six-man crews that rotated shifts to cover the job 24/7, and for all of this hard work we were paid seventy-six dollars a month. When I entered the work area, I noticed that the big Plexiglas map covered Russia, which was only seventeen miles from us. A Russian jet fighter base was located fifty miles from us, and in 1956 Russia shot down one of our planes over the Bering Sea.

I didn't see any women anywhere while I was on the tour, just 110 men, and I was going to be here for one year. I was assigned to one of the six-man crews and started work the next day. I would be scheduled to work seven days a week for my one-year assignment. Back then you didn't object to working seven days a week because this was before television, iPhones, and Xbox to play war games; we had our real war with Russia to keep us busy.

Enrolled in College

I HAD BEEN at my radar site for a few weeks, and I had some spare time to fill. Through the Air Force educational program we could enroll in some college courses offered by the University of Maryland. Everything was done by mail; we didn't have the Internet back then. I enrolled in algebra and English classes and started receiving my assignments in the mail. I worked on the assignments and sent them back through the mail system. This could take a long time because of bad weather when the mail planes couldn't fly in or out. Sometimes I would be doing my homework and one of my buddies would come by my room and say, "Let's go down to the PX and have a beer." I was just starting to like beer, so that sounded like a good idea, and my homework didn't get completed. One of the other problems was that I couldn't talk with anyone if I had questions about a homework assignment. We were so remote that the only way we could talk to anyone in the United States was with the help of ham operators. This was a shortwave radio system that could patch you to a landline. It didn't always work, so after long delays with the mail service and not being able to talk with anyone about my assignments, I decided to put my college days on hold and go down to the PX and have another beer.

We had lots of hobbies on our base. The one I liked was photography, and we had a lab for developing our 35mm film. We used 35mm film because that was what we used in the radar room so it was free. I enjoyed taking a picture and then watching it develop in the solution. I still have lots of the pictures I took fifty-nine years ago. We also had a radio station for our own listening, and the Eskimo village seven miles away could also listen to our radio station. I could work there and play the music I wanted to hear, so I spent many hours as a DJ playing my music and delivering the news that we could get from the Armed Forces Radio station in the United States.

Long Nights

WHEN I FIRST arrived in Tin City, Alaska, it was mid-November so the sun disappeared and we wouldn't see it again until spring. We had twenty-four hours of darkness every day, which can get to be depressing. I knew nothing about the surrounding area or what it looked like, so I would have to wait until spring to do any exploring around our base. Everything was done inside of our building except the snow-melting job; sometimes you looked forward to doing it just to get outside. On the reverse side of the twenty-four hours of darkness, we got twenty-four hours of sunlight in the summer. That was great when we were working on the second shift.

We would get off work at midnight, drive over to the airfield, and play baseball the rest of the night. I was glad to see spring arrive so I could get outside and explore the area. It was difficult walking because of the tundra, and we couldn't walk along the shore because the broken ice was piled so high. We still had snow on the ground, so I could have checked out some cross-country skis, but I had never done any skiing and was afraid to try it on my own. If I got hurt while skiing, it could be a big problem because there were no roads for EMS vehicles to pick you up. We had one road that went from our base to the airfield, which was about a half mile. We also had a road that went down to the shore of the Bering Sea. That road was used when we received a shipload of supplies for the base, and the ship was only scheduled for one trip per year. When I was there, we ran out of supplies and had to eat K-rations, the same ones that were used in World War II. In each K-ration package, we had a meal and always a pack of Camels. Since I had quit smoking when I was twelve years old, I gave my Camels to one of the guys who did smoke. When the large ship arrived with our supplies, the crew needed extra help unloading the cargo, so anyone who wanted to earn some extra money could help. I made more money working five days than the amount I was paid for working a month in the US Air Force. We had to stand in line and give our name, rank, and serial number (AF13593636) to get our seventy-six dollars a month—in cash.

The Tin City Mine

BEING FROM WEST Virginia, I was interested in mining, and at one time tin mining was done in the area where our base was located. There was an abandoned tin mine located about a half mile from our base. One day, after my crew got off work, we walked over to the mine to explore inside. Before we left the base, the other crew that was working warned us about the abandoned mine, noting that the inside of the mine was a favorite place for bears to hibernate for the winter. I think that thought was on our minds as we walked on the rugged path over to the mine. There were four of us making the trip, and we had our guns with us, but I always thought that I could run faster if I didn't have my gun to carry. As we approached the entrance to the mine, we had our guns at the ready for anything that might come out of the mine. We walked just a short distance into the mine and may have gone deeper, but after the other crew told us about the possibility of bears being inside the mine, we changed our plan about going any farther. So we had been inside of the tin mine, but it was not like the coal mines back home.

On our trip back to the base, we did some hunting for the willow ptarmigan, the state bird of Alaska. Back in 1957 Alaska wasn't a state. The ptarmigan is a good-tasting bird to eat, much like a pheasant. Since we were a small Air Force base and out at a remote site, the military rules were relaxed, so if we killed any birds, we would be able to go into the mess hall and cook them for ourselves. These ptarmigan didn't like to fly, so we were able to shoot them while they were still on the ground. We killed six birds, and when we got back to our base, we cleaned all of them and were ready to fix a good meal. Since I had a lot of cooking experience at home, I was elected to cook the birds. Of course I had never cooked anything like a ptarmigan, but it looked like a chicken without its feathers, so that is how I fried it, along with some mashed potatoes and gravy. We didn't have a cookbook to tell how to prepare a ptarmigan, but it all tasted good to me.

Sergeant Byrd

ONE OF OUR crew leaders was a career military man named Robert Byrd. He was a veteran of World War II and had been in the army before joining the Air Force. He was also one of the few men who had survived the Death March of Bataan. Of course, he was older than most of the crew members who worked in radar operations, and the younger guys looked up to him. He was the sergeant in charge of radar operations and was well-respected by all. He was the one who got me involved with photography. We used to go out on the ice and take pictures of seals and pictures of how the broken ice along the shoreline would be piled up so high. All of the film and other supplies for our photograph work were provided by the base, so we developed many pictures while we were stationed at Tin City.

There was an Eskimo village seven miles from our base, but it was off-limits to us. At one time some of the Eskimos took care of all the KP duties on our base, but before I got there, the base commander put a stop to that practice. So we did all of the KP duties ourselves. Sergeant Byrd, another crew member, and I went to see the base commander for a pass to visit the Eskimo village. Much to our surprise he gave us the pass. You could take a seven-mile walk over the top of a 2,200-foot mountain or try to navigate along the shoreline of broken ice. We chose to try the mountain, but it was a very rugged terrain with lots of snow still on the mountain. It took us eight hours to complete the seven-mile trip. We met with the people who were in charge of the village; they worked for the US government. Both of them were teachers, a man and his wife from Carlisle, Pennsylvania, who had three kids. They invited us to spend the night with them, so we did. The next day we were taken around the village to see how the Eskimos lived. They had small tar paper shacks with a cookstove, kitchen table, and sleeping quarters. The Eskimos had just returned from a seal hunt and were in the process of cleaning their seal, not a very pleasant smell in their house.

The houses smelled like seal because the Eskimos were cutting up the seal on their kitchen tables. They would get seal oil and use it for a number of things, such as burning the lamps to light up their homes. In the winter, the Eskimos didn't take a bath but instead rubbed the seal oil on their bodies to protect their skin. I would think girls could use the seal oil for birth control because they didn't smell very attractive after rubbing the seal oil on their bodies, but maybe the Eskimo boys loved that smell. The Eskimo people were friendly and invited us into their homes and offered us something to eat. I was glad to get the opportunity to meet the Eskimo people.

On the second day of our visit, we were supposed to start our trip back to the base, but there was a big storm blowing off the Bering Sea. With very high winds and more snow falling in the Eskimo village, the leader of the village said we shouldn't try going back to our base in those conditions. We had no way of contacting the base to let them know we were snowed in and would be late in returning to our base. The leader of the village seemed to be happy that we would be staying longer just so he would have someone to talk to, and we were glad as well. We had more time to take pictures, and this was the first time that any of us had seen a girl in a long time. I was starting to get used to the smell of seal oil when the weather cleared up after the second day of the storm, and it was time for us to leave our new friends.

We decided that because there was more snow in the mountains we should walk along the shoreline back to our base. It was not going to be easy no matter which route we chose. So the three of us said good-bye to the Eskimos and started our seven-mile trip over the broken ice along the shoreline. Again it was an eight-hour trip as we had to climb over broken ice and make sure we didn't fall and get hurt. The base commander wasn't happy when we reported to him. He told us that we could be court-martialed for going AWOL, but he understood why we could not get back in time.

P2V Neptune

THE P2V NEPTUNE was the only American naval land-based patrol plane, and it was used in 1957 for maritime and antisubmarine patrol. These were the planes that the navy used to patrol the international border between Russia and the United States. We tracked these planes every day on our radar screens and usually never made radio contact with the pilots. One day while I was on duty and we were tracking the P2V plane, we noticed that the pilot had gotten off course and was in Russia. We weren't the only ones to notice this, and the Russian Air Force scrambled three fighter jets toward the P2V plane. The pilot made contact with us, and we gave him directions to get back on the US side of the border. He was anxious because he had jets on both sides of him. He flew over our radar dome, and the Russian jets stayed with him. Even after the P2V plane continued on his patrol, the Russian jets continued to circle our radar dome. At that time our base commander put us on high alert, and we were all issued lots of ammunition and had guards all around the perimeter of the base. The Russian jets made one last circle around our radar dome and headed back to their base fifty miles away.

As I said before, the US Air Force was not trained to fight, so lots of the guards we had around the base perimeter were clerks, mechanics, cooks, and radar operators; our biggest fear was that we would shoot each other. I had shot at a lot of squirrels in West Virginia but never had shot at another human being. I think if someone was pointing a gun at me, though, I would not have a problem with trying to shoot them first. Our base commander kept us on high alert for two more days and then it was lifted as things got back to normal. In 1956, the year before I was stationed in Tin City, Alaska, the Russian Air Force had shot down one of our P2V patrol planes just off the coast of Saint Lawrence Island, which was located about a hundred miles from us in the Bering Sea. There was another radar site on that island, and we worked with the crew there to plot the aircraft traffic flying along the international border between Russia and the United States.

Arkie

WHEN YOU SPEND a year with a group of airmen who have no place to go, you get to know the men very well. We would get new men rotating in and out as they had completed their year of duty on this remote site. One of the men who arrived at Tin City about the same time that I did was another hillbilly, from Arkansas. He was a mechanic working in the motor pool on all of the equipment we had on base. He was not too happy about being stationed on a remote site in Alaska. He would much rather be stationed back in Arkansas so he could get some of his family's moonshine to drink. He would do things to try to make the base commander think that he was crazy so he would get sent back to the United States. Our base commander was a large man from Texas, and he always talked about the Texas Bluebonnets and how beautiful they were. He held the rank of major but was very loose with the military rules of protocol. He preferred to be called "Tex," unless he had to do something in the military guidelines. When we weren't working, we spent a lot of our free time in the mess hall, especially in the winter. Arkie would sit by himself having a cup of coffee, and if he saw the base commander come into the mess hall, Arkie would start talking loudly with his imaginary friend so Tex could hear him. One morning Arkie was sitting not too far from me, and when Tex got close to his table, he yelled, "Watch out, Tex. You're going to step on my dog." Of course Arkie didn't have a dog, but he was always trying to convince Tex that he needed to be transferred back to the United States. It never happened, and Arkie spent his year in Alaska just as I did. Many years later, as I watched the TV program *Mash*, I always thought that the writers of that show must have known Arkie to come up with the character Max Klinger, who was always trying to convince his base commander that he was crazy and should be shipped back to the United States. Arkie never wore women's clothes to try to convince Tex that he was crazy, and I don't think that it would have been a good idea around a hundred men who hadn't seen a woman in a year.

Sputnik

ON OCTOBER 4, 1957, the first artificial earth satellite was launched into orbit by the Soviet Union. When Sputnik was launched, it marked the start of the space race between Russia and the United States. Sputnik 1 was about the size of a beach ball, only twenty-two inches in diameter and about 184 pounds, and it took about ninety-eight minutes to orbit the earth. In a mad rush for the United States to catch up with Russia, the first satellite launched by the United States was on January 31, 1958.

Russia launched the first Sputnik before I arrived in Tin City, Alaska, but then Russia started launching more Sputnik satellites, and after a few orbits of the earth, the satellite would fall out of the sky. One of those satellites was projected to fall somewhere in Alaska. So we were all assigned to satellite watch duty. We took our rifles with us and set out on the tundra under a star-filled sky, watching for a flaming satellite falling out of the sky. No one in our group ever spotted a falling satellite. One did fall in Alaska but not close enough for us to observe.

Back in West Virginia, a ninth grade student at Coalwood

Junior High School was so impressed with the launch of the first Sputnik satellite that he wanted to become a rocket scientist. He and three of his buddies started building rockets and firing them up into space. They became so good at designing rockets, they entered the science fair for high school kids and won first place. This young science enthusiast graduated from college and then served in Vietnam. After returning from Vietnam, he started working at the space center in Huntsville, Alabama. Later he would write a book about himself and his three buddies building rockets when they were teenagers; the book was titled *The Rocket Boys*, and it became so popular that there was a movie made based on his book. The movie was called *October Skies*. When I saw the movie, it was the first time I saw people in the theater stand and cheer. It was such a good feeling that one of the kids from my high school followed his dream and became a rocket scientist—and it was inspired by the launch of the first Sputnik satellite back in October 4, 1957.

Short-Timer's Chain

SOME OF THE airmen stationed at the remote site made a chain out of paper clips, and it had 365 clips in it. They wore it hanging from their belt, and each day they removed one clip. Others, like me, made the short-timer's chain with only thirty clips hanging from the belt, which indicated that you had thirty days to complete your one-year tour of duty on this remote site. We would soon be getting our new base assignments, and we had no choice in where we were going. The US Air Force sent us where they had a need to fill in our classification, and so we were sent to fill those needs. The past year had gone by very fast because we were always busy working or doing one of our hobbies. We didn't have any towns close by that we could go to or any girls we could chase, but I think that the year of isolation was good for us. This was not so true for some of the guys who were married and had kids back home. Some ended up divorced; it was too much of a strain on their marriage. The isolation gave me lots of time to think about what I wanted to do with my life after I served my four years in the US Air Force.

The new base assignments were posted, and there was a

mad rush to find out where we would be spending the next three years of our life. Lake Charles, Louisiana, would be my next assignment. I knew nothing about the base, but my roommate, who was from New Orleans, would have traded with me if the Air Force would have allowed us to trade, but no deal. So he was off to a base in North Dakota. I still had seven more links in my short-timer's chain, so I went with a couple of my buddies out in the tundra to do some more ptarmigan hunting. We were successful in getting four birds and had another good meal that we cooked in our mess hall. Then we went down to the PX and had a few beers. We sat and talked about the last year that we had spent together, and now we would be going in different directions. It was good to be going home and seeing my family, but it was also sad that I would be leaving the friends I had made in Tin City, Alaska.

Take Me Home
Country Road

AFTER MY TOUR was completed, I had a thirty-day leave before I had to report to my new assignment in Lake Charles, Louisiana. I was flown back to Seattle, and from there I flew to Wichita, Kansas, to visit with my brother Dennis and his wife, Beverly, whom I had never met. They also had a daughter named Donna. Dennis was the only one of the Evans brothers who had made a career in the US Air Force, and he was stationed in Wichita, where he met his wife. Dennis had also requested a thirty-day leave, and we would be driving his car back to West Virginia to see our dad and then up to Michigan to visit our family members who had moved there. It was also the first time that anyone in our family would meet Beverly and Donna. I spent a week in Wichita. Dennis and I and some of his buddies from the base went squirrel hunting. The night before we were to leave for West Virginia, Dennis went to bed early, but I stayed up with his father-in-law. I did a lot of talking and too much drinking and got very little sleep. Dennis and I were sharing the driving, and when it was my time to drive, I fell asleep at the wheel. It was a good thing that Beverly was watching because she yelled at me and I was able to get back on the road without having an accident. Then, as Dennis was sleeping, I got us lost in East St. Louis, not a good place to get lost in at night. Dennis took over the driving and was able to get us back on the correct highway. We made it safely back to West Virginia, and our dad was so happy to see all of us. He got to meet Beverly and hold another one of his granddaughters. After not seeing me for a year, Dad even gave me a hug. We spent some time with Dad and then went to visit the Blankenship family. Clarence, Ernest, and Wayne were gone from home, but Shelby and Anita were still in school; plus the family had grown since we moved to Atwell back when I was in the ninth grade. Ida and John Blankenship had three more kids for a total of eight. After a good visit with the Blankenships, we loaded the car and headed north to Michigan to see our sister Irene and brother Walter and their families before we had to go back to our military life.

Lake Charles, Louisiana

AFTER I REPORTED to my new base in Louisiana, I could tell that I needed to make adjustments to my military life. We were a very small group of airmen up in Alaska, and the military rules were much more relaxed than they were here. I had to remember that when I met an oncoming officer, I had to salute him. The base was so much larger, and there were B-52 bombers taking off and landing most of the day on some training mission. The town of Lake Charles was very nice with lots of good Cajun restaurants. Cajun food would become one of my favorites, second only to biscuits and gravy.

After I got settled in, I made some new friends whom I worked with and started to adjust to my new surroundings. Our radar site was a few miles from the main base, and we rode a military bus to and from work. If you had a car, you could drive to work, but most of the guys rode the bus because gas cost money. Since we didn't earn very much money, we wanted to save it for girls and beer—and Lake Charles had plenty of both.

While growing up in West Virginia, I went to a segregated school, and I don't remember ever having any problems between black and white people. In Lake Charles in 1958 things were much different. I found that out quickly when my buddy and I went into a bowling alley. He was a black kid from Chicago, and when he and I walked into that bowling alley, everyone looked at us. Then three men came over to me and said, "You'd better get that boy outta here or both of you will be in trouble." I was surprised and hurt because I wasn't raised that way. We went back to the bowling alley on the base where we bowled a few games.

Some of my other buddies had cars, and we started cruising the drive-ins, hoping to pick up some girls. Just like in fishing, you catch some and sometimes they get away. One night I was lucky and caught a beautiful girl. It was her first night out with the other girls because she had a daughter about two years old and now she was ready to get back into the dating game.

Ella

I MET ELLA when my buddy and I were cruising one of the local drive-ins. We started talking, and I noticed how easy on the eyes she was. She was a tall, slender, blue-eyed blonde with a very pretty smile. She worked for a local doctor and had her own car, which was handy because I didn't have a car of my own. We started dating, and she would come on base to pick me up to go out for the evening. After not seeing a girl for almost a year, do you know how great it was to hold a beautiful girl in my arms again? I thought I had died and gone to heaven. She knew that I loved Cajun food, so one day she picked me up, took me to her apartment, and cooked a big pot of shrimp gumbo. Lord have mercy, now I knew that I was in heaven.

When I first arrived in Lake Charles, we got paid every two weeks and I would go downtown and have a big bowl of shrimp gumbo. Then my buddies and I would go out to the bars. I would always drink too much, throw up, and lose my shrimp gumbo. I soon learned that it was much better going out with Ella and having my shrimp gumbo; plus the perks were greater.

Ella's mother and dad kept her two-year-old daughter most of the time, but Ella usually had her on the weekends. So, when I didn't have to work on the weekends, I would go over and help Ella take care of her daughter.

The radar operation ran 24/7 with three crews manning the operation. We rotated about every five days, which made it hard to get adjusted to sleeping and also hard to get free time to be with Ella. She wanted to spend more time with me, but I had my responsibilities on the job. We dated for about six months and then parted ways because I think she wanted a husband to help her raise her daughter. I was only nineteen years old at the time and not ready to take on such a big commitment. How do you get over a broken heart? Find another girlfriend, and there were lots of them in Lake Charles, Louisiana. I went back to cruising the drive-in.

The Trash Can

MY CREW WAS scheduled to work the midnight shift for the next five days. One night my buddy and I had been out to the bar drinking before going to work. That was not a good thing to do because you could be court-martialed if you fell asleep on the job. So I went into work not feeling any pain, but the other crew members saw the condition I was in and knew they had to cover for me. One of them came up with the idea of hiding me in one of the large garbage cans, so they picked me up and placed me inside. It wasn't long before I was sleeping like a baby. We had extra men on each crew who could fill in if anyone was sick. After sleeping for a few hours, one of my buddies came to check on me and saw that I was awake. He looked up and down the hallway to make sure that our leader wasn't around, and then he helped me out of the garbage can. After a few cups of coffee and washing my face in cold water, I was able to do my job for the rest of our shift. I didn't want to be stuck in another garbage can because it didn't smell very good in there and people threw trash on me. I never went drinking before work again.

When my crew had to rotate, we would have some time off from work. We would get our girlfriends and have a party out in the swamp, which wasn't the smartest thing to do because the swamp had lots of poisonous snakes. We would get some hot dogs to cook over an open fire and some beer to wash them down. We did more of the washing down than we did of the eating. We usually got drunk, and when you are drunk, you do stupid things. We would go out into the swamp water and swim. Did you know that is where the water moccasin snake likes to swim? One of our crew members, a hillbilly, was in the water swimming, and we noticed a snake swimming up behind him. We yelled to let him know about the snake, and he disappeared under the water as the snake swam by. He came up and was able to grab the snake behind its head in his bare hands. Sometimes I think that the good Lord looks out for drunks and fools.

Boys' Town

ONE DAY AFTER work we were sitting in a bar drinking and one of the guys said we should plan a trip to Mexico. He had been there and said it would be fun trip. So we made plans, and each one of us requested a three-day pass from our base. There were five of us going, and one of the guys had a 1952 DeSoto that we would be traveling in. It was going to be a long trip. We drove through Houston, Texas, and San Antonio, Texas, and then headed south to Del Rio, Texas. Across the Mexican border from Del Rio was a town called Ciudad Acuna, and it was referred to as "Boys' Town." After a twelve-hour trip, we had arrived in Mexico, This little town had dirt roads, and on the day that we got there, it was raining; the main street was a big mudhole. As we were getting out of the car, a guy came riding a horse down the middle of the road. He was drunk and yelling that he had just bought this horse. We found out later that he was an airman from another base and couldn't take the horse back with him, so he gave it back to the Mexican he got it from. I am sure he didn't get all of his money back and often wondered how many more times that Mexican sold that same horse to a drunk wannabe cowboy. We didn't bring any extra clothes or even a toothbrush because we were only staying one day.

It was late Saturday night, and we were sitting in a bar filled with Mexicans. I think they knew that we had spent most of our money, so they started chanting, "Yankee, go home." We knew enough about history and how the Mexicans outnumbered the men inside the Alamo that we decided to drive back across the border into Del Rio, Texas. We parked on the street about 3:30 a.m. and fell asleep in the car, only to be awakened by the sound of church bells at about 7:00 a.m.; we had parked in front of a Catholic church. All of the people walking by on their way to church saw what a mess we were. I often wondered if the priest that morning preached in his message on the sin of drinking too much and making an ass of yourself.

The guy who had planned our trip to Mexico was older than the rest of us in the car. He was a loner, didn't drink, and spent most of his time reading books. He was from California and had worked in a pharmacy before joining the US Air Force. After we arrived at our base in Lake Charles, the owner of the car saw him take off the hubcap on one of the rear wheels. He had bought some drugs in Mexico and taped them to the inside of the hubcap. The owner of the car wasn't very happy because if we had been caught at the border, he would have lost his car and we would all be sitting in a Mexican jail eating Spanish rice and refried beans.

When my crew was working the day shift, we had a favorite bar where we liked to hang out. They had a good young country singer who was just getting started in the music business. We often took our girlfriends there because we were allowed to dance and the girls loved this new country singer. The singer was Mickey Gilley, and he would go on to become one of country music's biggest stars. You only had to be eighteen years old to drink in Louisiana, but some of the girls we took to the bar were only fourteen years old and we were about eighteen or nineteen years old.

One of my buddies sang and played the guitar, and he was good enough to get a job singing at one of the local bars. He was from Monroe, Louisiana, and his favorite country singer was George Jones. We sometimes went as a group to give him moral support and help him get his singing career started. One evening another buddy and I had been duck hunting in the swamps. We stopped by the bar where our buddy was singing, and there in the front row was a drunk Cajun who was making fun of our friend and telling him that he couldn't sing. He wanted to hear some good Cajun music and told our friend to get off the stage. My buddy and I went over to the Cajun and told him to sit down and shut up or we were going to kick his butt and throw him out of the bar. He wasn't very happy; however, after that he was not so loud but still drunk. My buddy and I got up to leave, and the drunken Cajun followed us out to our car; he wanted to fight. My buddy was sitting in the car at this time, and he got his shotgun and placed it under the nose of the Cajun; I didn't know a Cajun could run that fast.

My Own Car

I HAD JUST been promoted to airman second class and was now receiving $120 per month for my work in the US Air Force. Now that I was going to be paying for gas, I was upset because the price had jumped three cents right after I bought my car. Gas was going to be sixteen cents per gallon. One of the guys in our barrack had been in the Air Force for four years and was getting a discharge and going back home to Chicago. He had a 1953 Chevrolet that had been in a rollover accident, and the entire left side of the car was scratched up. It looked bad but ran well, and he let me have it cheap. I now had my own car so no more double dating or borrowing someone's car to go on a date.

One evening after work my buddy and I were cruising around town in my new car, and we pulled into our favorite drive-in where we parked next to a carload of girls. We started talking with these girls all from an all-girls Catholic high school. They asked us to come to a party at one of the girl's house the next weekend. We were given the home address, and after we finished talking to the girls, we drove to that address.

There were beautiful homes in a very nice neighborhood. Most of these homes belonged to the military officers from our base. Saturday came, and when we arrived at the party, there was a large group of guys and girls. We were invited in and told to get something to drink. There was a beautiful dark-haired girl who had dimples when she smiled, and just by the way she carried herself, I knew I didn't have a chance at dating her. We talked for a long time, but I never had the courage to ask her out; I didn't want to be rejected. I found out later that her dad was a general on base. So I moved on with my drink in my hand, and I met another beautiful girl. Her name was Barbara, but everyone called her Bobbie. We sat and talked, and I got up enough courage to ask her out for next weekend; much to my surprise she said yes. I found out that her dad was a major and a pilot flying a B-47 bomber. When I met her parents, her dad was friendly toward me, but I didn't get the same feeling from her mother.

An Officer
and a Gentleman

BOBBIE AND I had been dating for a few weeks, and I had started going to the Catholic church with her on Sunday when I wasn't scheduled to work. Every time I picked her up at her house, I could tell that her mother wasn't very pleased with Bobbie's choice of a boyfriend. After all, I was just an enlisted airman, and she wanted Bobbie to start spending more time at the officers' clubhouse. There she might find a young lieutenant who was an officer and a gentleman, who would make her mother happy. Bobbie was happy with me, so we continued dating much to her mother's dismay. Bobbie was born in California, and her family didn't sound like the local folks when they were talking. Being from West Virginia, I had a southern accent, which I think was one of the reasons that her mother didn't like me. For the first time in my life, I felt like I wasn't good enough for some people. Bobbie's dad and I got along, and I used to take her brother fishing with me along with some of my buddies from the base. You can bet that her mother was not going to get a Mother's Day card from me.

Bobbie and I used to go to the drive-in movies a lot. It was very hot in Lake Charles in the summertime, so we needed to roll down our car windows. When we did this, the mosquitoes ate us up. There was a product called Pic that was used as a mosquito repellent; it was in a coil shape and you lit it with a match and set it on your dash. It would smolder, supposedly to repel the mosquitoes; sometimes I think it attracted more mosquitoes. You sure didn't want to remove any of your clothes in those conditions.

Just about every Friday night, the Catholic High School Bobbie attended held a dance, and we danced to one of my all-time favorites songs, "Unchained Melody" by the Righteous Brothers. Those days with Bobbie were the best times I had while stationed in Lake Charles, Louisiana.

A Phone Call from My Dad

ONE EVENING I was lying on my bed in our barrack when someone down the hallway yelled, "A phone call for Roger Evans." I thought it might be Bobbie asking me to come over to her house. When I picked the phone and said, "Hello," a man's voice spoke, but I didn't recognize who it was. He said, "Your mother is coming home. Would you like to come home and meet her?" I just about dropped the phone. I had no idea there was any possibility that she would ever be released from the mental hospital where she had spent the last nineteen years of her life. After I was able to collect myself, I told my dad that I would try to get a two-week leave and come home. I told the officer in charge about my news from home and that I would like two weeks' leave. He granted my request so I started making my plans. I chose to take the train back to West Virginia, so I would be able to get up and walk around as I was traveling. Sitting was difficult because I had too many questions on my mind. I was twenty-one years old and had never seen my mother; I didn't know what she looked like. We didn't have a car, so we were unable to visit her, and we didn't own a camera, so we didn't have any pictures of her. I was two years old when she was committed to the West Virginia State Mental Hospital in Spencer, West Virginia. I was going home to meet my mother for the first time that I would remember.

On that long train ride from Lake Charles, Louisiana, to West Virginia, I thought of so many questions to be answered. The biggest one was if she was going to blame me for her illness. It happened not long after I was born. What did she look like? Did I look like her? Since we didn't have any pictures of her, I had formed a mental picture in my mind of what I thought she would look like. Would that mental picture be true? I was excited when my dad called, but I was also frightened because I didn't know what to do when I met her. Should I shake her hand or give her a hug?

As I sat on the train watching the telephone poles whiz by, I started thinking. Do I want her in my life? I had a very happy childhood without her, and now she was coming back into my life. What changes would she make? How can you love someone you don't know? Yes, she brought me into this world and gave me life, and for that I was truly grateful, but I just didn't know if I had a place in my heart for her. Then, as I was thinking about her, I wondered why tears were running down my checks. Maybe I did have a place in my heart for her. Could it be just a natural bond between a mother and child? If I ever needed God's help, it was now more than any other time in my life.

After almost three days of traveling on the train, we arrived in Bluefield, West Virginia, at 5:30 a.m., and I was scheduled to go by bus to War, West Virginia. The bus wasn't scheduled to leave until 8:30 a.m., so I didn't want to sit there the rest of the night. I saw a cab parked on the street and went to ask the driver if he would drive me to my house. He didn't know where Atwell was located, but he said that he had been to War. I asked him how much he would charge to drive me home, and he said he couldn't tell me until we got there. When we pulled up into my dad's driveway, I asked what I owed him and he said $13.20. I pulled out my wallet and found that I had a total of $13.80. Being the big tipper that I was, I gave him everything I had.

Mother and Dad were already out working in the yard, pruning an apple tree. When I walked up to them, I was a little disappointed when I first saw her. She wasn't anything like the mental picture of her I had formed in my mind. She had no teeth, her hair was a mess, and her dress was torn and tattered. Nothing like my mental picture. But nineteen years in a mental institution had not been kind to her. My dad said, "This is your mother." We just looked at each other and said hello, no handshake or hug. I just didn't know what to do or say. She had only been home for a week, so there were lots of things we needed to do for her. Dad had a set of false teeth made for her and we checked on her eyes, but there was nothing they could do to improve her eyesight since the hospital had performed the "ice pick" operation on her and clipped the optic nerve.

Slowly I was able to make eye contact with my mother, but what was I going to talk about with her? She wasn't aware of the events of the day, and I don't know if she could remember any of us kids and or what had happened to her nineteen years ago. So if I saw that she was looking at me, I would just smile, not knowing what to say.

I took my bags and went into my old bedroom, but something was missing. Gone were all of my clothes, my Big Creek High School yearbook, and all of the pictures I had collected over the years of the kids I went to school with. Also missing was my BC sweater with my varsity letter on it. Things like that can't be replaced. I had a chance to talk with my dad alone and asked him where all of my things were. He said that my mother was cleaning out my room and took all of my things and burned them. Dad wasn't aware of what she had done until it was too late. Again the thoughts came back into my head that she was blaming me for her illness and that she wanted to get rid of anything that belonged to me

This was a big change for my mother, being home and having the freedom to do as she pleased. She might have felt more comfortable in the controlled environment where she had spent the last nineteen years. We were never given a case worker to help Mother get adjusted in her new home. Dad seemed to be happy to have Mother at home, but I was still having a hard time dealing with it. Looking back to that time, I think that it would have helped if we'd had some type of counseling by someone from the hospital. I would have liked to ask someone there if my mother ever talked about her family or asked to go home.

In the short time that I had left before I had to report back to my base, Dad and I made sure that Mother was cleaned up and brushed her hair every day. The only makeup that she wanted was a jar of Noxzema; I guess that is what she had in the hospital and it worked. She had the most beautiful skin. Before I left, I was able to talk with her, and that mental picture I had formed in my mind was starting to develop into a beautiful portrait of my mother.

I rode a bus back down to Lake Charles and was glad to get back and see Bobbie. She had graduated from high school and would be enrolling in McNeese State College in Lake Charles. Bobbie and I went to a movie, and after the movie we went to our favorite drive-in so we could talk. She wanted to know how my trip back home went, and I told her that I wasn't sure how things were going to work out with my mother; I didn't know what to talk about. Bobbie's mother was still trying to get her to spend more time at the officers' clubhouse, but she wanted no part of that. We spent the rest of that summer hanging out at the beach and going to the movies.

I went to the officer in charge of our barracks and asked him about enrolling in college; I wanted to go to McNeese State. He told me what I needed to do to get enrolled and that the Air Force would pay my tuition. When I went down to enroll, I was told that I had to take an entrance exam; it was about a four-hour exam. I didn't do so well in English but was okay in math. I signed up for an algebra class and an English class. I was able to get my work schedule and my classes set up so I would be able to do both. Bobbie and I would sometimes pass each other on our way to our classes, and I started noticing that she didn't seem to have the time to talk with me. I had only been in college for a couple of weeks, but I was already smart enough to realize something was wrong. She stopped and talked with me one day as we were going to our classes, and she told me that she was dating one of the football players from McNeese State. Did you ever go to class and never hear a word the professor was saying? That's what I did that day because Bobbie's news came as a shock to me; we had been so happy. Darn old football players. Well, that wasn't the first time a girl told me to "hit the road, Jack" and maybe not the last time. I continued going to my classes and always hoped that I would get to see Bobbie, but I think that she changed her path so she could avoid me.

There were rumors going around that our base was going to be closed and that we might be transferred to another base. Then we were told if we had less than one year remaining on our time in service that we might be able to get discharged early, or we could reenlist for four more years.

Stay or Go

THE RUMORS CHECKED out to be true: our base was closing. Not the B-52 bomber base but the 812 AC&W radar operation was being shut down at this base. I had just over six months to go before my service time would be completed, and I wasn't sure that I wanted to reenlist for another four years. I had one last thing to check on before making my final decision. I was going to apply for OCS (Officer Candidate School) if they would let me. When I checked on it, I was told that it required at least two years of college, and I stated that I was in college at the present time. They agreed to let me take the entrance test, and if I passed with a high average, I could apply. I was going to show Bobbie's mother that I was an officer and a gentleman. Also it might impress Bobbie; she was still on my mind and in my heart. However, I have never failed a test as badly as I failed that one. I was just glad that I hadn't told Bobbie I was taking the OCS test. There were lots of questions on the test dealing with calculus, and back in Big Creek High School, that class was never offered to us. I had taken all of the math classes that were offered in high school, but calculus wasn't one of them. After failing this test, I developed a fear of ever taking another test for the rest of my life.

So my decision was made: I would take the early out. With only six more months to serve in the Air Force, I had to start thinking about where I was going to live. West Virginia was out of the question because there was no work where I grew up; maybe I could get a job in a coal mines, but that was not in my plans. I talked with my sister Irene in Michigan, and she said that I could come and live with her and her family until I got a job. My brother Walter and Irene's husband, Clinton, both worked at General Motors; maybe I could get a job there. My brother Jerry had graduated from West Virginia University, and he too was working at General Motors. My brother Robert had also graduated from WVU; he was a chemical engineer working for BF Goodrich in Ohio, but he would soon move up to Michigan. It looked like the entire Evans family would be living in Michigan, so why not me?

Final Days in
the US Air Force

I WAS GETTING out of the Air Force six months early, but the time dragged by so slowly. My work kept me busy, but since Bobbie and I were no longer dating, I was lonely. I dated some other girls, but it just wasn't the same. At this point in my life, I just wanted to get my time in the Air Force over and move on to the next phase of my life. I was down to the last week before I would be packing my car and heading home to see my mother and dad and then completing my trip in Michigan. I received a phone call from Bobbie, and she wanted to go on a date before I left. I don't know how she knew that I was leaving, but I was glad to see her for the last time. We did a lot of talking and some of it was sad, but we were both glad that we could be in each other's arms for the last time. We would continue to keep in contact by phone and letters after I relocated to Michigan.

I left Lake Charles, Louisiana, the next morning after saying good-bye to Bobbie, and I was on the road. There were no expressways back in those days, so I had to drive through lots of large cities. I drove twenty-three straight hours before I pulled over on a country road somewhere in Virginia and took a nap. After a short nap, I was on the road again for another six-hour drive to my dad's house in Atwell, West Virginia. It was good to see my parents, and I could see an improvement in my mother. It was much easier for me to talk with her. I spent a week with them before I headed up to Irene's house in Ypsilanti, Michigan.

It was November 1960 when I was discharged from the Air Force, and the economy of the country was bad so it was difficult to find a job. I called my high school buddy, Roger Bellamy, who was living and working in Cleveland, Ohio, in a tool and die shop. He told me to come down and stay with him and look for work in the area. I did. I put in applications at many places, but no one was hiring at that time. Roger's girlfriend lived in Washington, DC, with three other girls from Bradshaw, West Virginia. He wanted me to go with him to see Sue because he was going to give her an engagement ring. Sue was very excited to get her ring.

Of the three girls living with Sue, I knew one of them from our high school days when Roger, Gerald, Kenny, and I went to Bradshaw just about every weekend. The other two girls were from Iaeger High School, but I had never met them. (I wish I had because they were very pretty.) It was New Year's Eve and Sue had made reservations for all of us to attend the party at a bar. It was very loud and very crowded inside the bar. We did a lot of dancing and drinking, and I know that I was still okay when the clock struck midnight and the kissing began. One of Sue's friends and I had started kissing before the traditional New Year's Eve kiss. I continued to drink more than I should have and didn't remember anything after 1:30 a.m., but the next morning I woke up in bed with just my underwear on. I don't know how I got there or who put me there. I just hoped that one of the girls took advantage of me.

It was time for Roger and me to head back to Cleveland because he had to go to work. I stayed another week with Roger and his family and got to spend a lot of quality time with his mother. I loved her because she had been like a mother to me since I was fifteen years old and had moved to Atwell. Roger's sister Brenda was graduating from high school, and she was getting married after graduation. It was hard to believe that she was getting married because it seemed like just yesterday I had given her a first kiss when she was twelve years old and had a toothache. Roger was happy that he had given Sue the engagement ring, and he was doing well learning his tool and die trade.

I had no luck in finding work in Cleveland, Ohio, so it was back to Michigan for me. I went to several factories and put in applications, but still no one was hiring at that time. My brother Jerry was working at a General Motors plant in Willow Run, Michigan, and he told me the plant was going to be hiring new employees starting in April. Jerry was a supervisor there, so he got me an application to fill out and gave it to the front office for processing. I received a phone call telling me to come in for an interview at eight o'clock the next morning. I was nervous when I went in. The guy who interviewed me asked some questions and wanted to know if I still wanted the job. "Yes sir," I replied. "When can I start?" He told me to report for the second shift at 2:30 p.m. that same day.

First Day at General Motors

THE AIR FORCE was behind me now, but my military training was still with me as I started my first day of work at General Motors on May 2, 1961. My cousin Charles Evans was working at the same plant on the same shift, so we rode together to work. He was a spot welder on the assembly line, which was one of the hardest jobs in the plant. At this plant we were making the body for the Corvair, a compact car manufactured by Chevrolet from 1960 until 1969. We were producing sixty-eight cars an hour when I started working there. Then Ralph Nader wrote the book *Unsafe at Any Speed*, which caused a slowdown in our production schedule because the book was about the Corvair. Chevrolet discontinued production of the model in 1969.

There are many lessons that you learn in school, but the lessons that you learn in life will last for the rest of your days. I can still remember my first day of work at General Motors. I was young and dumb. I had bought a lunch box and a thermos bottle. The thermos bottle had a cork stopper in it. I fixed my lunch and packed it neatly in the lunch box and filled my thermos bottle with 7-Up. When lunchtime came, I sat down and opened my lunch box to find all of my food was wet with 7-Up. The fizz in the 7-Up blew the stopper out of the thermos bottle. Just like my lesson in life about sticking a knife in a toaster, I didn't forget this one either. I never made those mistakes again.

My cousin Charles was disappointed because he thought that I would be working as a spot welder just as he was. Instead I was given a job as a "trucker." When the Corvair bodies were assembled, if there were any mistakes in the assembly operation, the bodies would have to be pulled off the line for repair before they was transferred to the paint department. A trucker's job was to pull off the bad ones for repair, and once they were repaired, put them back on the line. There were two truckers, one at the front of the body and one at the rear.

Rolling in the Money

WHEN I WAS discharged from the Air Force, I was making $120 per month, but you have to remember that I was given free room and board. When I got my first check at General Motors, I couldn't believe how much money I was making. It was more than three times what I was getting in the Air Force. I was glad because I could start paying Irene rent every month. She had let me live there for free the first six months because I was unemployed. I opened my first bank account and was able to save some money each month. For the first time in my life this hillbilly from West Virginia was rolling in money.

My job was going well because I was a hard worker, and when my supervisor told me to do something, I replied with a "yes sir." One day my supervisor said to me, "Son, you don't have to talk that way to me," and I said, "Yes sir." Because I was such a hard worker and wanted to learn different jobs, my supervisor moved me to another position. I was going to be an overhead hoist operator. When the car body came down one line, it needed to be picked up and transferred to a line going in the opposite direction. One operator picked up the body, pushed a button on the control panel, and the body traveled on an overhead rail to the other operator who used the control panel to set the body down on a dolly traveling in the opposite direction. Everything was just a matter of timing because you had to set the body on four moving points. After a few days of training, I was able to do the job without any help. It was a very good and easy job that made me feel like I was landing a plane. I worked on this job for a few years, and then I was trained to do some welding on the inside of the body as it moved along the assembly line. After a short time on this job, I was moved back to the final repair hole where I had started as a trucker. Now I was going to be trained to do body repair work, which involved welding, soldering, and bumping out any flaws in the metal body. This was the highest-paying production job in the plant. I was glad to receive all of this training.

Babysitting

MY SISTER IRENE had three kids, and my other sister, Betty, also had three kids. Betty had moved from New Jersey with her family so she could be near Irene, and Betty's husband, Jack, wanted to get a better-paying job at General Motors. He started at the same GM plant where my brother Walter and Irene's husband, Clinton, worked. I was working on the afternoon shift, so I had a lot of free time in the mornings, which Betty and Irene took advantage of. They would go shopping, and I was left babysitting. On June 23, 1961, I was outside on a nice sunny day washing my car and babysitting the six kids. I looked up and saw two pretty girls walking toward me, and when they were next to me, they asked if I needed any help babysitting. We introduced ourselves; one was named Diane and the other one was Denise. Diane had short dark hair, big brown eyes, and dark skin, things I always liked in a girl. I had never dated a girl with those features, but when I had the chance, I asked her out. She said no.

I wasn't going to let Denise get away without asking her out, and much to my surprise she said yes. I noticed that

Denise had a foreign accent and found out that she was French, born in Montreal, Quebec, Canada. She and her family had moved across the street from Irene's house five years ago. I had seen these two girls walking up and down our street before but never had the opportunity to talk with them. I went over to meet Denise's family, her mother, two brothers, and one sister. Right after they came to this country, their father bought a new house and new furniture, and landscaped the yard. Everything was looking good but the marriage. He wanted a divorce. This was a very tragic event in their lives—being in a new country, not speaking the language very well, and now their mother would need to find a job. Denise's dad was a tool and die maker and always made his monthly alimony payments on time, but they needed him more to be their leader in this new country. I wasn't much help in trying to teach them the English language because I was from West Virginia and struggled with the language myself.

Denise Legault: 1962, High School Senior

Roger Evans: 1960, Air Force

Boblo Island

DENISE AND I started dating, but we couldn't go anywhere in the evening because I was working the afternoon shift. Only on the weekends could we go to a movie or some other event. All summer long we got together. We went for long walks down to Prospect Park or drove over to the Chick Inn Drive-In to eat before I had to go to work. The Chick Inn Drive-In is still open today with their carhops, and that was sixty-five years ago. I bought my first new car after Denise and I started dating. It was a 1961 Corvair, made where I worked. Denise didn't know how to drive a car, so I spent the summer teaching her how to drive a stick-shift car. It wasn't easy teaching her how to work the clutch, but I had experience from teaching my dad the same thing. It was a lot more fun teaching Denise.

When we were dating, one of the popular places to go on a date was Boblo Island. It was located eighteen miles up the Detroit River from the city. Boblo Island was an amusement park, and you had to take an excursion boat up the river to get there. The park had two boats in service, and each boat would hold 2,500 people. There was a live band on the boat and a big dance floor. It was a good place to take a beautiful girl and try to impress her. When we got to the island, we walked around the amusement park and got on a few of the rides. Then we went over to the food court to get something to eat; it was the first time I ever had french fries with malt vinegar on them, and they were very good. After we ate, we went back to the rides. I don't remember the name of the ride we were about to get on, but it was a big round cage where you stood up with your back against the wire cage. The cage would rise up into the air and start spinning, and all of a sudden the bottom would fall out from under your feet but you were held in by the centrifugal force. I don't do spinning; I get sick when I am spinning, but I couldn't throw up while spinning because of the centrifugal force. I started screaming like a sissy and wanted to get off. When the ride stopped, I started throwing up all over Boblo Island. I don't think Denise was too impressed.

Her Senior Year

DENISE WOULD WALK over to Irene's house and help me do the babysitting, or I would be over at her house. We spent the entire summer together and had a lot of long walks. When we went anywhere, we always were holding hands, and one day I told her that after fifty years of marriage, I would still be holding her hand. That promise was kept. Summer was coming to an end, and Denise would be going back to school to finish her senior year. I was still working the afternoon shift, so I would drive to school and pick her up for lunch each day. Most of the time we went to the Chick Inn, or I picked up food from Bill's Hot Dog Stand and we went to Prospect Park to eat and kiss. Bill's Hot Dog Stand is still open today, sixty-five years later. I used to get some dirty looks from lots of the high school guys because I was there every day to pick up the prettiest girl in their school. The first winter that Denise and I were dating, we frequented Prospect Park where she was teaching me to ice skate. Skating was part of her life in Montreal, and she was good. She was able to teach me how to dance on ice skates. I wouldn't want to enter any ice dancing competition, but I did enjoy dancing with Denise.

It was springtime and we had talked about getting married after Denise's graduation. She and I went to meet her dad, and I asked him if it would be okay if I married his daughter. We had met before, and I think that he was okay with her choice of a boyfriend. He gave his approval for me to marry Denise. She wanted to get married in the Catholic church, but since I was not a Catholic, we could not get married at the main altar. I also had to attend classes, and we had to sign papers saying that we would raise our kids in the Catholic church. I was raised as a Baptist, and I found out what a big difference there was between the two churches. It didn't matter to me; I would jump through hoops, run through hell, or do whatever I needed to do to marry Denise. She was a very special person who had brought so much love into my life, and I never wanted to lose that love.

*Denise Legault at her first Catholic communion
in Montreal, Canada.*

June 23, 1962

WE PICKED JUNE 23 for our wedding day because it was exactly one year after we first met. I was twenty-three years old and she was eighteen years old at the time. I had completed my classes at the Catholic church, and we were getting married at St. John the Baptist Catholic Church in Ypsilanti, Michigan. It was a beautiful day for the wedding, and we had about seventy-five to one hundred friends and family attending the ceremony. Before I left for the church, I got a phone call from someone I hadn't heard from in a long time. It was Bobbie, and she asked what I was doing. I told her that I was getting married in three hours; she had no idea because we hadn't talked in a long time. She wished me well and lots of happiness. After the wedding, we had a reception at Denise's house and then went to northern Michigan for a short honeymoon. We had purchased a new trailer for our first home, and we lived in the trailer park for about three years before we bought our first house.

After we had been married almost eight months, our son Tony was born. I was always told that the first baby can come at any time, but the second one takes nine months. There was no way we could say he was premature because he weighed ten pounds, twelve ounces. After he was born, Denise tried breast-feeding him, but because he was so big and hungry all the time, she wasn't able to keep doing it. She went into postpartum depression, which lasted for a long time. I am glad that Tony was such a good baby so it didn't add any more stress on Denise. She started getting better about the time Tony was walking. One other thing that added stress to her life was that I was still working the afternoon shift and she didn't like being alone after dark. One night, as she was walking down the hallway to the bedroom, some man was opening the door to sneak into the trailer. She screamed and the guy ran away, but she never got over that fear. We wanted to buy a new house so we could get away from the trailer park, and I started working two jobs to earn extra money so we could afford it. I got a job in landscaping and worked in the morning before going to GM.

Denise and I on our Catholic wedding day, June 23rd, 1962.

Denise's first trip to West Virginia 1964

Dad's Retirement

MY MOTHER HAD been home about three years and was improving to the point where she could help Dad with the cooking and cleaning. In 1963 my dad had a bad accident while he was working on the railroad. He broke his leg and was unable to work for a few months, and during that time Mother, with the help of their neighbors, took care of Dad. After my dad's leg had healed, he went back to work, but he was having a hard time doing his job so he retired after working for forty-seven years on the railroad. Since all of us kids had migrated up to Michigan— except Dennis, who was still in the Air Force, and his family— my parents sold their house in West Virginia and moved to Michigan in 1964. We were a very close family, and we all lived with in twenty-five miles of Mother and Dad.

Just about every Sunday the entire family gathered at our parents' house for dinner, and that continued for many years. Walter, Robert, Jerry, and I had a standing tee time every Sunday morning, but our dad had never played golf. So we got him a set of clubs, and he started playing with us. After all, I had taught my dad how to drive a car, so I should have been able to teach him how to drive a golf ball. Not true. But the score didn't matter to my dad; he was just happy to be playing golf with his boys. My brothers Walter and Jerry had bought a hunting cabin in northern Michigan, and we started deer hunting together in 1963. When my dad moved to Michigan, he also started deer hunting with his boys. Today Jerry, Dennis, and I are still deer hunting with our kids, sons-in-law, and grandkids, and this tradition has lasted fifty-three years. In November 1969 we were deer hunting up at the cabin, and all of us boys had to return home to go to work, but Mother and Dad stayed at the cabin so he could hunt longer. Mother stayed in the cabin while Dad was out in the woods hunting. One morning he was late getting back to the cabin, and Mother started to worry. Then she saw him walking toward the cabin, dragging a big buck he had killed. He had to drag the deer about three-fourths of a mile, not an easy job for someone who was sixty-nine years old. He and Mother loaded up his deer and drove back home.

The Crowded House

IN 1965 DENISE and I decided to sell our trailer and buy a new house. Washington Square was a new subdivision near my parents' house, and we went to check it out. We found a model that we liked and could afford, so we made a down payment to get the construction started and were promised that we would be able to move into our new house by the first of January. Denise was pregnant with our second child and due around Christmastime. We put our trailer up for sale, and it sold much quicker than we expected. So we had to move out before we wanted to.

My dad said that we could move in with him and Mother. They had a four-bedroom house, so Denise, Tony, and I moved in with them. At the same time, my brother Jerry and his family were in a similar predicament; they were buying a house with no place to live for a short time. Dad invited them to move into his house as well, and there were now eight of us living in the same house. Back in West Virginia, there had been nine of us living in a much smaller house with no indoor plumbing. It was okay for Jerry and me, but Denise and Millie (Jerry's wife) didn't feel the same way. Still it was only going to be a short time until our house was supposed to be completed. We all celebrated Christmas together that year, and Denise was very pregnant. I took her to the hospital on December 29, 1965, and she had a beautiful baby girl, Pamela Denise Evans, weighing nine pounds, twelve ounces. Denise again suffered from postpartum depression, but it didn't last as long as the first time. She was depressed because there were so many people living in the house and she didn't have the privacy she would have liked after having a baby. We were able to move into our new house in early February. It was wintertime, and I was working only at General Motors, so I was able to help Denise take care of the babies and help with the housework. Spring was near and I would be working two jobs again. The guy I worked for in the landscaping business had the contract to do the final grade work for all of the houses in our subdivision.

Yard Work

WE HAD MOVED into our new house and Denise was starting to feel better, glad to have time alone when she wanted it. I was busy trying to do things around the house and working two jobs. If I could go back in time, I don't think I would have worked two jobs, but I was only trying to make a better life for my family. Since the landscaping company was doing work in my subdivision every day, the owner asked me if it would be okay to leave some of the equipment in my yard. So the crew would come to my house, and we would start our job from there. I worked out a deal with the owner to do the landscaping for my yard. We planted trees, shrubs, and flowers, and then the sod was delivered. We laid it on a long, hot day and I was very tired. After the crew left, Denise brought me a glass of iced tea and told me how nice the yard looked; then she wished me a happy anniversary. Oh my goodness, I had completely forgotten our fourth anniversary on June 23, 1966. It never happened again in our fifty-two years of marriage.

We were the first homeowners in the neighborhood to have our yard landscaped and new sod installed, so all of the neighborhood kids came over every day to play in our yard to avoid playing in the dirt. I think all the kids in our yard caused some stress for Denise because she felt responsible while they were there.

I wanted to get a pet for Tony and Pam, but Denise wasn't sure if that was the right thing to do. Her family had lived on the second floor of an apartment building in Montreal and never owned a pet of any kind, so she was afraid of dogs and cats. I talked her into getting a dog and a cat for the kids; I'd had pets all of my life. We got a toy collie and a baby kitten. Denise was still having a hard time trying to adjust to the pets. I was still working the second shift and came home after work one night to find Denise standing up on a chair. She thought that the baby kitten was attacking her, but the kitten had only wanted to play.

Baby Number Three

DENISE FINALLY ADJUSTED to the dog and cat that we had gotten for the kids. Once she got over her fear, she loved the animals, and we had pets for many years while our kids were growing up. Denise started having severe headaches, but the doctors couldn't find anything that might have caused them. She was pregnant and expecting our third child. Tony and Pam were excited because they were going to have a new brother or sister. I just wanted a healthy baby because Denise had a rare blood type, Rh-negative. When you are pregnant with this blood type, the chance that something could go wrong with the baby increases. We were all happy on August 11, 1967, when Gail Marie Evans completed our family. Gail would have a hard act to follow because Tony and Pam were such good babies.

Well, she didn't live up to their examples because she had to be held all the time; if you laid her down, she would cry. Denise and I spent the first three months of Gail's life carrying her in our arms. I don't know about Denise, but I was getting depressed, even thinking about trading her in for a cold-nosed puppy. We somehow survived those three months and were glad that we hadn't traded her in because she was a very good baby after the rough start.

We had a new house and a beautiful landscaped yard in a nice subdivision, but something was not right with Denise. She didn't like living in a subdivision and having people come over to visit unannounced. She always felt like our house wasn't clean enough when people dropped by. She wanted to move to a place where she had more privacy. We started looking and found a tri-level home with four acres in Bellville, Michigan. We put our home up for sale, and it sold in a very short time. When we moved into our new home, the owner still had three horses and a pony on the four acres with a horse barn. He said that if we let his three horses stay there until he got his new barn built, we could have the pony. We agreed and now owned a dog, a cat, and a pony. One day, however, Denise was out in the barn brushing the pony, and he stepped on her foot. She gave the pony back to the owner.

Something Is Wrong

WE WERE ENJOYING our new house in the country. We had a big garden area and were getting so much produce from the garden that we started canning green beans, tomatoes, and a few pickles. Denise was starting to lose weight and sleep a lot. I was always taking her to our family doctor, and on one of our visits, he recommended that she see a psychiatrist. He made an appointment with one of his doctor friends—I will call him Dr. Gordon—and he would be Denise's doctor for many years. After a few appointments with Dr. Gordon, Denise still wasn't getting any better. She had deep depression and slept most of the time. I started doing more around the house so I could help Denise with the cooking, laundry, and general housework. None of that seemed to matter. Denise was still having a hard time; she just couldn't overcome her depression.

I had been working for seven years at General Motors and was still working on the afternoon shift. I did not have enough seniority to work on the day shift. I was thinking about quitting and doing some other type of work so I could be home with Denise in the evening. I didn't know if that would make her feel better, but I just didn't know what else I could do to help her. My brother Walter told me that the plant where he worked was going to give the Skilled Trades Apprenticeship test, and he wanted me to take it. So he helped me brush up on math problems to get prepared for the test. I went to his plant, took the test, and was interviewed after the results were in. I had a good score and was offered an apprenticeship as a millwright. I had wanted to be an electrician, but because of the Affirmative Action program, the electrical apprenticeship went to two black guys who had lower scores than I did. I was just happy that I would be learning a trade and hoped to have a better future. The apprenticeship program was a three-year program, and I would be going to college during that time. I was transferred from my plant to the one where my brother was working as an electrical engineer.

The First Time

I WAS OFF from work for the December holidays and enjoying my time with Denise and the kids. All holidays were special to my family and me. Denise was involved with our church and made sure that the kids were with her every Sunday morning. We were married in the Catholic church and had signed papers saying we would raise our kids as Catholics, but we never went to a Catholic church after we were married. Denise went to the Baptist church with me and liked it so much that she was baptized there. Denise's dad had told me that one of the reasons he left Canada was because of the Catholic church. He said every Saturday morning the priest would come by and encourage him to have more kids so there would be more Catholics. The priest also told her dad not to let his kids learn to speak English. He wanted them to speak only French.

Denise was not getting any better with the medication that Dr. Gordon had prescribed for her, and during a visit with him, he recommended that she be committed to Mercywood Psychiatric Hospital, where he worked. There was no way that she was going to let them put her in the hospital. My first thought was is she going to spend the next nineteen years in a hospital just like my mother had? I didn't want any part of her being in a psychiatric hospital. Dr. Gordon was able to calm us down and explain that she would only be there long enough for them to get her on the correct amount of medication so she could function at home. Denise was willing to give it a try and agreed to be committed; this was the first of thirty-four times that she would be in and out of a psychiatric hospital in our fifty-two years of marriage. Each time I had to put her in the hospital that same thought came to mind: am I going to be like my dad and not have my wife around to help me raise our kids? I was very lucky to have my mother and dad come and stay with us when Denise was first committed to the hospital. They took care of our kids while I was at work. Over the years my sister Irene also played a big part in helping me with the kids when Denise was in the hospital.

The Worst Pain Ever

IN 1969 DENISE was committed to Mercywood Psychiatric Hospital for the first time, and she was diagnosed as manic-depressive (later that name would be changed to bipolar). Our kids at that time were very young and still needed lots of attention; Gail was still in diapers. Denise was in the hospital for six weeks that first time. I had just started my Skilled Trades Apprenticeship program, was working lots of overtime, and was going to college. My workload had increased at home and at work. After Denise was released from the hospital, it wasn't long before she had to be recommitted. I was able to bring her home for a few hours to visit the kids, and then I had to take her back. One day, as we were getting ready go back to the hospital, Pam was crying and did not want her mother to leave. She wrapped her arms around Denise's leg and wouldn't let go; she was crying and begging her mother to stay with her. That was the most emotional pain I ever experienced; it turned into physical pain in my heart, hurting for Pam. Even today, as I try to write about it, the image is so vivid in my mind that tears are running down my face. There is nothing worse than watching one of your kids hurting for the love of his or her mother. Something that I never had was the love of my mother.

Over the next few years, Denise was in and out of the hospital. It never got any easier when I had to take her to the hospital because I never knew when she would get out, or even if she would get out. Our kids were getting older and didn't require as much work to take care of them. Thank goodness, I didn't have anymore diapers to change or wash. Back in those days, the diapers were cloth and you had to wash them and reuse them, not a pleasant job.

Denise would be doing good on the medication that her doctor had prescribed, and then a lady at church would tell her she didn't need that medication; all she needed was God. Each time Denise would end up back in the hospital. Maybe God was working through the doctor to help Denise.

Electroshock Therapy

DENISE WAS GIVEN electroconvulsive therapy (ECT). This is a procedure, done under general anesthesia, in which small electric currents are passed through the brain, intentionally triggering a brief seizure. ECT can cause changes in brain chemistry that can quickly reverse symptoms of certain mental illnesses. To be successful, most patients need six to twelve treatments to do away with depression. I don't recall how many treatments Denise had, but they didn't work for her. It did, however, block out her memory of a lot of things in her past. Dr. Gordon continued to adjust her medication, and there was new medication coming out to help people with bipolar disorder. Denise had been with Dr. Gordon for a few years, and she liked him; he was doing a good job in treating her. When we had an appointment with him, he would talk with Denise first and then have me come in and talk about how I thought she was doing. He also would ask me lots of questions as if he was looking for answers.

One Friday afternoon we had an appointment with Dr. Gordon and again he was asking me lots of questions. I never expressed my feelings about Dr. Gordon to Denise, but I felt that something was bothering him. When I picked up my newspaper on Monday and turned to the obituaries, I saw that Dr. Gordon had died suddenly over the weekend. We found out later from our family doctor that he died from a gunshot to his head. He was bipolar and had shot himself. That was hard for Denise to take because she had looked up to him, put her faith in him, and was hoping that he would be able to get her out of this bipolar world she lived in.

She was so depressed that she had to go back into the hospital. She was assigned to another psychiatrist—I will call her Dr. Mary—and Dr. Mary was also a professor at the University of Michigan Medical School. Denise liked Dr. Mary because she was the first female doctor she'd had. After working with Denise and me for a few months, Dr. Mary asked if we would come to her class and talk about being bipolar and living with someone who is bipolar. I left that decision up to Denise, and she said yes, we would talk to her class.

Speaking at the University of Michigan

THE NIGHT BEFORE we were scheduled to speak to a class of future doctors at the University of Michigan, I don't think that Denise or I slept very much. We were thinking about the type of questions we would be asked. In the back of my mind, I thought that because we were at the university, we were going to be graded on our answers. Dr. Mary told us to relax and talk about our lives and the problems we encountered in living with bipolar disorder. When we walked into the auditorium, we were surprised to see how large the class was; there were between one hundred and 125 students in this class.

Dr. Mary introduced us to the class and gave a report on what she knew about us and what she had observed since she became Denise's doctor. Dr. Mary asked me to talk about living with someone who was bipolar and the problems that it could create. I started off by telling the class about my childhood and growing up without my mother, who was in a mental hospital for schizophrenia. I also told them the lessons that I had learned from watching my dad raise seven kids without the help of his wife. Mother had spent nineteen years in the mental hospital, and I never met her until I was twenty-one years old. I told the class some of the things that Denise had done, how she acted when she was depressed, and how different she was in the manic state of mind.

After I finished, Dr. Mary allowed the class to ask questions of Denise or me about our life. Denise answered a few questions, and I could tell something was wrong with her. Then a girl asked me, "She said in a marriage where one person is bipolar that ninety-five percent of the time the marriage ends in a divorce. After the things you have told us, how are you still married?" I told her about the things I had learned from my dad, that you don't just give up. My mother or Denise didn't ask to be this way; it was how they were born. Just like my dad, I was going to be there for Denise when she needed me. I also made a promise when we were married that I would be there through sickness and in health. Then I turned to face Denise and told her that I was still here because "I love you very much."

The Gandy Dancer

AFTER THE CLASS ended, lots of the students came up and thanked us for coming to their class and talking about bipolar disorder. Dr. Mary gave us a gift card to eat at the Gandy Dancer restaurant in Ann Arbor. The Gandy Dancer was the old railroad station, which was over one hundred years old and made of large stone blocks. It is rated as one of the best seafood and steak restaurants in Ann Arbor. Denise and I went to the restaurant, got a table, and placed our order. I could tell that something was troubling Denise, and I asked her what was wrong. She started crying and said she didn't know about the things I had talked about and wasn't aware that she had done them. Then she asked me why I hadn't left her; again I told her how much I loved her and the thought of leaving her had never entered my mind. This was the reason I left the decision up to Denise about speaking before Dr. Mary's class. Denise seemed more relaxed after I talked to her, and we both enjoyed a very good meal at the Gandy Dancer.

We had been living for about three years in Bellville, where we had four acres of land and raised a beautiful garden each year. Because Denise was in and out of the hospital so many times and we didn't have any family members close by, we thought about moving closer to our family. Most of them were living in the Hamburg, Michigan, area. We went to see a builder and purchased a one-acre lot located in the woods. We had looked at some other houses and liked one we had seen. I took that floor plan and made some changes to it, drew it up, and asked the builder to construct a house like that for us. We agreed on the price, and he started building on April 1, 1973. We moved into our new house on August 1, 1973. At that time I was working seven days a week and going to college, and we would visit the building site every day. It was good that we checked because when they dug the basement, it was in reverse. We called and the next day they made the correction. They had told us we should be able to move into our new house by July 15. It didn't happen.

Sold

WE CHECKED EVERY day on the progress of our new house and tried to time it so our existing house would be sold when we were ready to move into our new house. When we lived in Bellville, Denise's family lived closer to us than my family did. Denise's sister, Cecile, used to come and visit with us, and her brother Johnny and his wife, Cathy, would also visit. I had bought a second car so Denise could get out of the house and visit her mother. Denise's mother had to go back to work after her divorce, and she was working at Eastern Michigan University. She had started out working in the cafeteria, but she had done a lot of secretarial work back in Montreal and was very good at shorthand, which was required back in those days. She was afraid to try to get into that field of work because it was all in French back in Montreal. Her kids kept encouraging her to talk with the people in that department. She was interviewed and took a test and was hired as a secretary to one of the deans. She worked there for several years before she retired. While I was at work, Denise would visit with her mother and take the kids so they could spend time with their grandmother.

It was time to put our house up for sale to make sure it was sold before we moved into our new house. The day that the real estate agent put the For Sale sign in our yard, one of our neighbors came by and bought our house. We were going to have to move out before our new home was finished. We had a twenty-foot camping trailer and got permission from our builder to set up our camper on site so we could live there until our house was ready to move in. We were hooked up to the electricity, water, and sewer system, and we had some of our furniture stored in the garage. We hooked up our refrigerator so we could store more food in it; it was much larger than the one in our camper. Denise always looked at this time as being very hard on her because she was stuck inside the camper with three kids while I was at work or school. She also said that some of the workers were stealing things out of our refrigerator.

Our New House Is Ready

ON AUGUST 1, 1973, our new house was finished and we were ready to move in, especially Denise. She'd had enough of living in a twenty-foot camping trailer with our three rambunctious kids. We had lived in the camper for six weeks. We bought some new furniture and appliances, so the inside was set up, but the big job was outside. I worked in the yard, getting it to final grade, removing some of the trees, and getting ready to lay sod. I still had too many trees in our yard, and it would take four hours to cut the grass because I had to mow around them. I would later cut down sixteen trees, and I had a contractor come in and cut down thirty-eight more. After removing all of those trees, it took me only two hours to mow the grass.

I had completed my Skilled Trades Apprenticeship program and was a journeyman millwright. I worked in the maintenance department, and it was a seven-day-a-week job. I had completed my college courses but would go back later and take special classes, such as robotic training at GMI, ductwork design at the University of Toledo, and a Dale Carnegie course on public speaking. I had more time to be at home so I could help Denise raise our kids and continue to work on our yard. We really enjoyed living in our new house and being able to see so much wildlife in our yard. We would see deer, wild turkey, foxes, coyotes, coons, squirrels, rabbits, and many different types of birds in our yard. We had two snowmobiles, and in the winter we could drive out of our garage into ninety acres of woods. Denise rode the snowmobile until one day when she got excited and ran into the side of a block wall. She tried to stop but gave the machine more gas when she should have been applying the brake. That was the end of her snowmobile riding. Tony was old enough to drive a snowmobile, so I would take him along when we rode with my brother Walter and his two sons-in-law. In the winter Denise always loved having a fire burning in the fireplace, sipping a cup of hot chocolate, and watching the deer out in the snow.

Tony and Football

WHEN WE MOVED to Hamburg, Michigan, in 1973 and into our new house, the Hamburg Recreation Department was just starting a new football program for younger kids. Tony was going to be in the sixth grade. Size and weight determined what level you would be playing in, and Tony was a very big boy for his age. When we signed him up to play football, he was placed in the top level with some kids who were in the ninth grade. There is a big difference in the maturity of a sixth grade student and a ninth grade student, so this made Tony nervous. Every day, just before practice began, Tony would get sick and throw up. So he told Denise to start making spaghetti because that was easy to throw up. That first year of the football program I helped with the coaching and continued doing so until Tony was playing football in school. My brother Robert and I had a Little League baseball team that we coached for a few years too. Robert's two boys, Mark and Steven, played on the football team with Tony, and all three would play together during their high school years. Mark would go on to play football for four years at Adrian College.

All of the years that Tony participated in football, basketball, track, and wrestling, Denise didn't attend very many of his events. She was suffering from too much depression and didn't want to be around other people. Many years later Denise and I started spending our winters in Texas. As we were driving down there, I looked over at Denise and she was crying. I asked her what was wrong, and she said that she was thinking about Tony and all of the games that she had missed. She wished that she could have been a better mother. I tried to explain to her that she was a good mother and that she did the best that she could do under those conditions.

Denise enjoyed our new house, but she was still having bouts of depression and at times needed to go back into the hospital for a few weeks to get her medication changed. She was working with a new psychiatrist, whom I will refer to as Dr. Ken.

Tony Evans, senior year football season with Denise and I.

First Attempt

DENISE WAS STILL battling depression and couldn't do any work around the house, so I was doing most of the cooking for supper. The kids were getting old enough to fix their own breakfast, things like toast and jelly or cereal. After I left for work, Denise would go back to bed and sleep most of the day. I would call and check on her to make sure that she was okay and try to encourage her to get up and get out of the house, go visit a friend, or go shopping. One day I called, and when she answered the phone, I could tell that something was wrong. Her words were slurred, and I was having a hard time understanding her. I kept asking her what was wrong, and she would say that she was okay. Then, after I asked for the third time what was wrong with her, she admitted that she had taken an overdose of her medication. I hung up the phone, ran out to my car, and was on my way home, a twenty-five-mile trip. I was driving one hundred miles an hour and wasn't going to stop, even if a cop pulled up behind me. In fact I was hoping that one would follow me home. I got home and Denise had passed out, so I got her into our car and drove to the emergency room at St. Joe's Hospital in Ann Arbor. They rushed her in, and when I explained what she had done, right away they started pumping her stomach. When they were able to get her stabilized, they recommended that I get her back into the psychiatric hospital. That I did, and she was there for about three weeks. Dr. Ken was able to get her out of her deep depression by adjusting her medication.

After we got her back home, I pleaded with her to never try killing herself again. I told her that she had three beautiful kids and a husband who needed her. I said, "If you ever feel that desperate, come talk to me. I am always here for you, and we will get you some help." She promised me that she would do that. This was her first attempt at committing suicide, but unfortunately it would not be the last. Depression is a very hard thing to control, and it can take over your life to the point where you don't want to live anymore.

Mistakes I Made

OF THE THIRTY-FOUR times Denise was in the hospital, most of them happened when our kids were small. Later, after the kids were gone from home, she went ten years without being admitted to the hospital. When the kids were small and she was in the hospital, I made lots of mistakes as I look back now. I wanted to make it easy for our kids, so I tried to do everything by myself. I used the TV to keep them entertained; I used the TV as a babysitter and hoped that it would keep their minds off of their mother. When I was doing the housework, Pam always came and helped me while Tony and Gail watched TV all day. I guess you could say that Tony and Gail were not afraid of work because they could sit by it all day and not be afraid of it. I think that Pam thought if she helped me clean the house, her mother would come home sooner. I also made a mistake by not emphasizing that they do their homework, but I didn't want to add anymore stress to their lives. They still did well in school.

When I was growing up and my dad had to raise seven kids alone, there was no TV for us to watch to help keep our mother off our minds. I was so young that I never missed her because I never knew her; she was admitted when I was two years old. Plus things were so much harder back in those days; there was no way my dad could do everything by himself. Each one of us kids were given chores to do each and every day. We had to cut firewood for cooking and bring in a bucket of coal for heating the house in the winter. One of the houses we lived in didn't have running water, so I had to get water for cooking and drinking every day. More water trips were necessary when it was time to take baths or do the weekly laundry. In the spring all of us kids had to dig up the garden plot with hand tools and plant our potatoes, tomatoes, cucumbers, onions, and sweet corn. We learned lots of valuable lessons back in those days, and the best lesson was that we didn't want to do things this way when we got older; we wanted to get an education.

Vacations

WHEN I WAS growing up, my dad could never afford to take a vacation. We didn't have a car so we couldn't have gone anywhere. My dad did take a few days off every September to go squirrel hunting with the Blankenship family. We had to carry all of our camping equipment on our backs to wherever we were going to camp; most of the time we camped up in Warriormine holler. As kids we looked forward to this every year. We would have a campfire every night and sit around the fire listening to our dad and John Blankenship tell tales about their childhood. They were born in 1900, and as kids they had to worry about Indians attacking them when they were out hunting. I am not sure how much of that is true, but back then around the campfire, it was the gospel. Hunting was something that our dad passed down to his five boys, and it is something that we still do as a family. April first was the opening day of trout season, and we always camped up at Big Creek Scout Campgrounds. Our dad wasn't on these campouts; it was Dennis, Clarence, Ernest, Wayne, and I, plus about one hundred other campers. Opening day of trout season was a very big event and one that we enjoyed very much as kids.

After Denise and I got married, we took a vacation every year, and we did that for the entire fifty-two years we were married. We took our kids to such places as Disneyland, Sea World, Cedar Point, Daytona Beach, Fontana Village, and Rocky Mountain National Park. The most relaxing vacations we had with our kids were up at the hunting cabin that my brothers Walter and Jerry owned. We went up there for a week every summer with our kids. We fished in the Rifle River and took the kids to Tawas City so they could go swimming in Lake Huron. It was about twenty miles from the cabin in Omer, Michigan. Denise always enjoyed the vacations we spent at the "Pot of Beans," the name Walter gave his hunting cabin.

My Father's Advice

AS I WRITE this, Father's Day is coming up, and it made me think about some of the best advice my father gave me so many years ago. It was about the second time that Denise was put back into the hospital for depression. The kids and I were not adjusting very well with her not being at home. My mother and dad were staying with us so I could continue to work. I was still working the afternoon shift and would get home about midnight. One night when I came home, my dad was still up. We sat down at the kitchen table and started talking. I asked him how my kids were doing and if they were doing what he asked them to do. He said the kids were great, but I think he would have said that regardless of how they behaved. I told my dad that I didn't know how much more of this I could take. It was hard to go to work and worry about Denise and wonder if she was going to be in the hospital for a long time like Mother was. He told me that I needed to turn it over to God, and he would see me through the hard times. He also told me to have more patience. He said he had waited nineteen years for his wife to come home, and that was a result of his strong faith in

God. When you have seven kids to raise by yourself, you don't have time to sit around and feel sorry for yourself. After listening to my dad tell me what he had been through, I felt like crap for complaining about Denise being in the hospital for ten weeks. I tried to live by the advice my dad gave me that night.

As my dad and I were sitting at the kitchen table talking, my son Tony walked into the kitchen in his PJs. Dad and I could see that Tony was sleepwalking. He stopped in the middle of the kitchen, pulled out his penis, peed on the kitchen floor, laughed, and went back to bed. My dad and I just looked at each other and couldn't believe what had just happened. I got the mop and cleaned the floor. My dad and I were afraid to wake up Tony while he was peeing on the floor because we were afraid it would scare the crap out of him. Next morning Tony had no idea what he had done.

The Church Lady

DENISE MET THIS girl in church, and they became very good friends and did a lot of things together. I wasn't very fond of this girl because I thought she was taking advantage of Denise; she knew that Denise was bipolar, and she told Denise all of her family problems. This girl had three kids and a husband who worked whenever he could. Someone who is bipolar likes to spend lots of money, and Denise did that. This church lady kept telling her that she couldn't afford to buy school clothes for her three kids. So Denise went shopping with the church lady and her three kids and used our credit card to pay for the kids' school clothes. Denise never told me what she had done, nor did she talk to me before she went shopping. When I got my credit card statement and saw the charges Denise had made, I asked her what they were for. Denise explained that the church lady needed help and we had money in the bank so we needed to help them. Denise had such a giving heart and was always trying to help someone who was less fortunate than us.

Denise and the church lady started going to visit patients in nursing homes around the county. They visited with the patients and sang to them, trying to make their life a little better. They did this for several years, and Denise was always driving her car and supplying the gas for these trips. Somehow Denise found out that our church was giving money to the church lady to cover the cost of the gas, but she never told Denise that she was receiving the money. When I found out what had been going on, I was upset because the church lady had been taking advantage of Denise again. I tried to talk to Denise about the situation, but she still wanted to give to people who had less than we did. I believe in helping others, but I also think that they should try to help themselves first. I didn't feel that the church lady was doing that, nor was her husband. If Denise loved you, she was your friend for life because of her unconditional love.

Denise was in the manic state of her bipolar illness, and she could be hard to control when she was like that. She was upset about something, and when I got home, I couldn't find her. I made a lot of phone calls, talked with our pastor to see if he knew where she was, and went driving to look for her. She never came home the first night, nor did she call to let me know that she was all right. The next day I went to the Michigan State Police Department to file a missing person report. I was told that I couldn't file a missing person report because she hadn't been missing long enough. Needless to say, I wasn't getting any sleep and was very worried about what might have happened to her. On the third day of her absence, I found the phone number of the church lady and gave her a call. When she answered the phone and I told her who I was, she got very quiet and didn't want to say anything. I asked her if Denise was there, and she said yes. I asked her to put Denise on the phone, and I was able to convince her that she needed some help. Denise agreed to let me pick her up and bring her home. I was able to get Denise back into the hospital, and the doctors were able to get her medication adjusted. About four weeks later she was released from the hospital.

I wasn't fond of the church lady from the first time she took advantage of Denise, and after this latest incident, I could never forgive her for what she had done. I felt that she should have called me when Denise was at her house because she could tell that my wife needed help. The church lady put me through hell for three days by not calling to let me know that Denise was at her house. Years later, when Denise and I talked about those three days, she would always tell me that I should forgive the church lady, but I never have and never will.

The church lady was the one who would tell Denise that she didn't need all of that medication, that all she needed was God. So Denise would quit taking her medication and always end up in the hospital.

In Control

DENISE DIDN'T LIKE that I was the one in control of almost everything involving our house. She wanted to be included in running the house and said that she would take over the banking, paying the bills, and planning our meals. Just to keep the peace and give her some responsibility, I let her try to do those things. It lasted about four months; she was not paying the bills and she was writing bad checks. It got to the point where I had to hide the checkbook from her. If we had extra money in the bank, she thought that we should be helping people who were in worse shape than we were. It was during this time that she started sending money to some of the TV evangelists whom she followed. One of them would cry as he was begging for money, so Denise was sending him money every month. One day, as I was watching the news, a video of this TV evangelist showed him coming out of a whorehouse, and I am sure that he was using my money to pay for the call girl. It was at this moment that I took control of our checkbook again. I didn't want to have to do that because it made Denise feel like she failed again. I tried to get her involved in other things so she would feel like she was contributing to running our household. When the depression returned, she lost all interest in doing anything.

The depression was getting worse, and one day she went shopping and was gone most of the afternoon. When she came home, she had a look of fear in her eyes. I asked her what was wrong. She told me that as she was driving God was talking to her, and she felt that she couldn't live up to God's words. She thought that she should kill herself, and the way she tried to do that was to drive her car head on into the approaching car. She drove toward the oncoming car, but the other driver was able to get out of her way. I am still thankful that she wasn't killed and that she didn't kill someone else. The depression continued to get worse, and she was admitted again into the hospital.

Each and every time I had to put Denise in the hospital I had the same fear. Would this be the time that she would never be released? I would always think about my own mother and the nineteen years that she spent in a mental hospital. After Denise's second attempt at suicide, I made up my mind that I couldn't be with her twenty-four hours a day. I had to depend on God and pray that he would watch over her when I couldn't be with her. After I prayed to God, my fear was gone. I was doing what my dad told me some years ago: just turn it over to God.

I was thankful at this point in our lives that our kids were old enough to take care of themselves. I don't think that I ever told them that their mother had tried to take her own life for the second time. It was still very hard on our kids each and every time I had to put Denise in the hospital. As the kids were growing up, I don't think they could ever have sleepovers at our house with their friends because we never knew how Denise was going to be. There were times when someone would come to visit Denise and she would go into our bedroom and close the door. I never had any of my friends come over after work because we just never knew how Denise would react.

My job required me to work seven days a week most of the time, and as I look back, I feel ashamed because I was glad to be out of the house. It is difficult to be with someone who is bipolar twenty-four hours a day. I know it wasn't her fault that she was bipolar, and she didn't enjoy living like that either. When Denise was depressed, she slept most of the day or just lay down because she couldn't function. The kids and I did the housework and prepared our meals and took care of the lawn. No matter how much you tried to talk Denise out of her depression, it didn't work. The only solution was to put her in the hospital so the doctor could adjust her medication and talk with her on a daily basis. She was in the hospital thirty-four times during our fifty-two years of marriage, and I think she spent a Christmas, a Thanksgiving, and an Easter in the hospital. Not a good place to be on those holidays.

Queen for a Day

AFTER I HAD completed my Skilled Trades Apprenticeship program, I was classified as a journeyman millwright. The program was set up as a four-year program, but because we worked so much overtime, I was able to complete the program in three years and three months. I was glad when I completed the program because I had no more school to attend and I could spend more time at home with Denise. After I worked three years as a skilled tradesman, I was offered a job as a skilled trades supervisor and would be on a salary; no more union dues would be taken from my check.

It was October, and all my brothers and our dad were in northern Michigan for a week of bow hunting for deer. On Sunday night, before I had to go back to work on Monday, I received a phone call from Bill, my general supervisor, and he asked me if I would like be a skilled trades supervisor. I told him that I would like to try that job, so he said to be dressed with a tie when I reported for work the next day. I got up and dressed in some nice slacks, a matching shirt, and a tie. When I entered the maintenance office, some of the guys had a look of surprise on their faces, and the superintendent came over to me and asked what I was doing there. I told him that Bill had called me the previous night and asked if I wanted to go on Supervision and told me to wear a tie to work. The superintendent said that Bill had left work early last Friday and some things had changed after he left. The superintendent told me to leave my tie on and work with one of the other supervisors for the day and then go back to my toolbox the next day. When I reported back to work the next day in my coveralls, a lot of the guys started calling me "Queen for a Day," and that lasted for a few months. That didn't bother me because I was just happy to be working, and most of all I had enough seniority that I could work the day shift and be at home with Denise and the kids in the evening. It had been a couple of years since Denise had been in the hospital, and my job was going great at the time. Life was good.

After all of the kidding I had to take from my coworkers, my general supervisor, Bill, came and talked to me. He apologized for his mistake and explained what had changed after he had left work the previous Friday. I was scheduled to be promoted, but because of the Affirmative Action program, they had to promote some black guys to Supervision. So for the second time, Affirmative Action affected my life. (The other time was when I was trying to get into the electrical apprenticeship program.) Will, one of the black guys who was promoted, was a very good friend of mine. He and I had gone through the apprenticeship program together, and he was a good supervisor and eventually was promoted to general supervisor.

A few months later I was called into the maintenance office by our superintendent, Paul, and he asked if I was ready to go on Supervision. Kidding with him, I asked if it would be for more than one day. He laughed and assured me that it would be longer, so I accepted the offer. Paul was not just my superintendent but he also was a deer-hunting friend of my brother Walt. In fact Paul was the one who got Walt into bow hunting, and then Walt got all of his brothers and our dad into bow hunting.

After I became a skilled trades supervisor, I worked in that job for two years. Then I was called into the office and asked if I would like to be an engineer. That was an easy question for me to answer. Of course I would. I liked the fact that I wouldn't be working so much overtime and could be home to help Denise. For the next ten years, I worked as an engineer for General Motors, and I worked in the same office as my brother Walt; he was the senior electrical engineer. I never finished my college degree because I had three kids who were involved in many different activities and a wife who needed me at home as much as possible. I was very thankful to General Motors for all of the opportunities the company gave me. That is why today I still buy GM cars.

Three Long Days

DENISE WAS HAVING a hard time and her mind was going into the manic stage of her bipolar illness. These times were always the hardest for me and the kids because she was getting high, just like someone on drugs. When she was like this, we couldn't control her and always had to put her back in the hospital. One morning she wanted to take down all of our curtains and wash them, but when she was in a manic state of mind, she would start several jobs and never finish any of them. So on that morning, I wouldn't let her take down all of our curtains and wash them. She got very upset and slapped me three times; each one was harder than the one before it. I made her sit down, and she started crying and saying that she didn't love me anymore. I went back into the family room to drink my coffee and watch the morning news. Then I realized that she had quit crying and it was very quiet in the living room. I got up from my recliner and went to check on her. She wasn't in the living room, so I began to search the house inside and out, but she was nowhere to be found.

After walking up and down the road in both directions for

about an hour, I gave up and went back inside the house. As I walked into our house, I heard the phone ringing and answered it. It was our neighbor Bill. He told me that he was driving to work and saw Denise walking, so he stopped and picked her up. He said that she seemed to be confused and said something about not wanting to be married anymore. Then she rolled down the window and threw something out. He also told me that he let her out at the Gandy Dancer restaurant in Ann Arbor. I jumped into the car and drove to the Gandy Dancer. I spotted her sitting at a table, and she had already gotten her food and was enjoying a very good meal. She didn't have her purse or any money with her, but she was still enjoying her food. When she saw me, she was happy and acted as though nothing had happened. She wanted me to sit down and order something to eat, but I told her that I wasn't hungry. After she finished eating, I paid for her food and we went home.

When we got home, I noticed that she didn't have her wedding rings on, so I asked her where they were. She said that she threw them away. Then her mind went on to other things that she needed to get done in our house. She wanted to rearrange the furniture in each of the rooms, paint the bedroom walls, wash the windows, wash the curtains, and do other smaller jobs. When she was high like that, her mind changed so fast and she couldn't concentrate on anything long enough to complete it. I couldn't get her to stop and go to bed at night; her mind wouldn't let her rest. When she was up all night moving things around in each room, I wasn't able to get any sleep either. I was always worried that she would do something and get hurt. When someone is in a manic state of mind, he or she is much stronger that a normal person.

One night Denise went down to our basement and carried up a heavy piece of furniture by herself and put it in our family room. I don't know how she was able to carry that furniture up the stairway by herself. Later I needed our son Tony to help me get it back down to the basement. Denise would stop what she was doing to fix herself something to eat, and then she would start some other project and forget that she had something cooking on the stove. I had to watch her to make sure that she didn't start a fire accidentally in our kitchen and burn down our house. She went for three long days without any sleep and had our house in a mess. She was putting things on the walls that looked good to her in her frame of mind but later would need to be removed. On the third night without any sleep, Denise was baking a cake at about 2:30 a.m. I had been lying in bed, trying to get some sleep, but I was up most of the night checking on Denise. I went into the kitchen to check on her, and her face was lying in the chocolate icing on the cake. She had been icing the cake when she passed out from exhaustion. I woke her up and cleaned her face and was able to get her to go to bed. The next day I got her back in the hospital. Then I had the big job of trying to get our house back to the way it was before those three long days.

New Wedding Rings

AFTER THOSE THREE long days without any sleep, Denise was back in the hospital. She would spend the next six weeks getting her medication adjusted so the doctors could bring her back down from her manic state of mind. It was Christmastime, and I wanted to get Denise a new set of wedding rings because she threw away the ones that she'd had since we were married. She wasn't aware that she had thrown them away. The ring set that I had gotten her back in 1962 cost $110, and I think it was an eighth of a karat. You have to remember that I had just started working and opened my first bank account, and it wasn't filled with lots of money. The new set of wedding rings that she liked cost $3,500—cost of inflation, I guess. She was happy with the new rings.

After spending six weeks in the hospital to get her back down from her manic state, it would be two years before she had to be hospitalized again for her bipolar disorder. During those two years, we enjoyed our life and each other. I was always thankful for the quality time that we got to spend together between her hospital stays. Ever since she had been diagnosed as bipolar, she took a medication called lithium, which is prescribed for all bipolar patients. It helps to stabilize the patient, but most of the time other drugs are used to help control the mood swings. With all of these medications in her system, it was hard for Denise to think clearly and she couldn't remember many of things that happened to her. Each medication she took had side effects, and after such a long time, the side effects built up in her system and caused other problems.

Denise had problems with her kidneys, and we found out later that the prolonged use of lithium could cause kidney failure. The doctors started giving her medication to help with her kidney problems because they wanted her to stay on her lithium. It was very important in treating her bipolar disorder.

Three in a Row

STARTING IN 1986, Denise and I lost someone in our family for three years in a row. My oldest brother, Walter, had been battling prostate cancer for over two years. Walt was like most men and wouldn't go to the doctor until it was too late. When he did go, he was told that he had prostate cancer and it had already started spreading throughout his body. He went to Canada for some experimental cancer treatment that did help him get better for a short period of time. He lost his battle with cancer in 1986; he was only fifty-nine years old, way too young. Losing Walt was very hard on me because he had done so much to help in my life and had taught me so much. He was the one who sat with me when I was five years old and lying in the hospital for six weeks with a broken leg. He taught me so much about deer hunting and fishing. Walt helped our dad hold our family together after our mother was committed to the mental hospital. Walt was our leader, and wherever Walt went, the rest of the Evans family followed. That is why we all moved to work and live in Michigan.

After Denise's dad retired, he moved to Daytona Beach,

Florida, and bought a motel. He lived there for several years, and Denise and I and our kids visited him. Once, when Denise wasn't doing very well with her depression, I put her on a plane and she spent about four weeks with her dad. He eventually sold his motel because he couldn't deal with all of the college kids who came down for spring break and left his motel in such bad shape. We received a phone call from one of his neighbors who said that Alcide Legault was in the hospital and wasn't doing very well. So Denise and I, along with her two brothers and their wives, flew down to Daytona Beach to be with their dad. He was in bad condition, diagnosed with cirrhosis of the liver, but he was not a drinker. He was glad to see his kids, and he seemed to be getting better when we had to fly back to Michigan. Denise's sister flew down to be with him when we left, and she called about five days later and said he had passed away. It was a shock to Denise and her brothers because we thought he was getting better when we last saw him. That was 1987; Alcide LeGault was seventy-seven years old.

My dad and mother had gotten to the point where they needed supervision twenty-four hours a day. My brother Jerry and his wife, Millie, lived close to our parents, and the rest of the family was paying Millie to watch over them. She had been doing that for a long time, but we thought that she should be paid for all of her work. As they got older and needed supervision 24/7, we got together and decided they needed to be in a nursing home. They were placed in a nursing home about fifteen miles from where most of us lived, and we went to visit them every Sunday, just as we had done when they were living in their own home. We would get together and fix dinner at their house every Sunday; our standing menu was fried chicken, mashed potatoes and gravy, pinto beans, and cornbread. That started in 1964 when Mother and Dad moved to Michigan and lasted until 1985 when we had to put them in the nursing home. Our dad was loved and respected by all seven of his kids and twenty-three grandkids. Sometimes I think that I owed my dad so much more that the other kids did because I was the youngest. And yes, I will agree with my siblings that I was spoiled. After my dad gave me a whipping for smoking when I was twelve years old, I think he knew that he was harder on me than he needed to be, and after that, if I did something wrong, he made me sit on the couch. My dad helped me so much when Denise was committed to the hospital, and I was able learn from him when we were growing up as he kept our family together while our mother was in the hospital. My dad lost his eyesight about a year before he passed away in 1988 of natural causes. He passed away in March, and in April he would have been eighty-eight years old. Even today I miss him and wish he was still here because when I have a problem, I would like to have someone to talk to. So today I do what my dad taught many years ago: I turn it over to God. I love and miss you, Dad.

Our Twenty-Fifth
Anniversary

DENISE AND I were married in the Catholic church back in 1962. Since I wasn't a Catholic, I had to take some classes, and we had to sign papers saying that we would raise our kids as Catholics. After we were married, Denise never attended a Catholic church. She started going to the Baptist church and liked the message that she heard each time she attended. She was baptized in the Baptist church and would remain a member for the rest of her life. She became very active in our church and started what she called her card ministry. She was always sending cards to people on the pray list and people who were having problems in their lives. Each card that she sent had some daily bread message in it or some Bible verse that she thought would be helpful to someone who was down. I used to think that the cards were a waste of time, but after she passed away, I had so many people tell me how much her cards helped them get through a hard time in their life.

The year was 1987, and Denise and I were going to be celebrating our twenty-fifth wedding anniversary. I asked her what she wanted to do to celebrate, and she said that she wanted to renew our wedding vows in the Baptist church with our three kids in attendance. We contacted our pastor and set it up for June 23, the same date we were married in the Catholic church back in 1962. After the wedding ceremony, we went to Niagara Falls for our second honeymoon. We stayed in that area for a week. Denise was so happy to be able to renew our wedding vowels in the Baptist church. When we got back home after the honeymoon, I told her that we'd had our Catholic wedding and now the Baptist wedding for our twenty-fifth anniversary but not to expect me to have a Jewish wedding on our fiftieth anniversary.

Our pastor, David Swink, had been so much help to Denise and me over the last several years. She would talk with him when she was depressed, and many times he was able to lift her out of her depression and prevent another hospital stay. We were so happy to have him in our lives.

Denise and I on our 25th wedding anniversary, after renewing our wedding vows.

Back As a Skilled Trades Supervisor

IN 1988, AFTER my dad passed away, I took a week off from work, and when I went back, my supervisor called me into his office. He told me that our superintendent wanted me to go back out on the floor to replace a skilled trades supervisor who was going to be out for back surgery. I had worked in this area, and they needed someone with experience working in the chrome-plating maintenance area. It was located on the second floor, where we chrome-plated most of the bumpers for all of the General Motors cars. Our plant was listed as the world's largest chrome-plating facility. The worst part about working in that area of the plant was that you were around lots of hazardous chemicals. Several employees who had worked in that area for a long time ended up with lung cancer from breathing the fumes coming off the plating tanks.

After the skilled trades supervisor had his back surgery and was cleared to come back to work, he was put in a different area, and I spent the rest of my employment in the chrome-plating maintenance area. I had a good crew of skilled tradesmen, and that made my job easy.

Not only was my crew a good group of skilled tradesmen but they also were young and good softball players. One of the engineers I had worked with was a good softball player, and I suggested that we each form our own teams and play once a week after work. Of course, if you are going to play softball after work, you need something cold to drink after the game, so beer it was. I played second base, and I was smart enough to wait until after the game to start drinking. I didn't want to have too much to drink and perhaps misjudge a line drive and catch it with my nose. My nose had already taken a beating from playing football with the black kids I grew up with, and in high school football we didn't have face masks on our headgear. Playing softball with my crew that summer created a better working relationship, and we got lots of compliments on how well we kept the plating line running. It was a good summer.

Ypsilanti State Hospital

AROUND 1980 DENISE had become out of control; she was in a very high manic state of mind. She needed to be in the hospital, but I couldn't do anything with her; she wanted to fight with me. I called Pastor Swink, explained how Denise was acting, and asked if he could come over and talk with her. He came over, and after talking with Denise for a while, he could see that she needed to be in the hospital. I called our private hospital to see if we could get her committed, but I was told that they didn't have any rooms available. Pastor Swink called the Ypsilanti State Hospital to see if we could get Denise committed there, and they did have some available rooms. Denise didn't want me to go with her to the hospital, so Pastor Swink and a lady from our church, who was a good friend of Denise's, took her to the hospital.

The hospital would not let anyone visit Denise for the first week she was there; the doctors were trying to get her medication adjusted. After that week, I was going to visit her and our youngest daughter, Gail, wanted to go with me to see her mother. When we got to the hospital, I was very disappointed.

It wasn't anything like the private hospital Denise had stayed in before. Ypsilanti State Hospital was a state-run mental hospital. When the staff found out who I was there to see, they went to get the doctor who was in charge of Denise. I talked with her doctor while Gail visited with Denise, right next to where the doctor and I were sitting. There wasn't a separate consultation room, just an area enclosed by privacy curtains. While I was talking with the doctor, we heard Gail scream. The doctor and I jumped up, pulled back the curtains, and saw a young black guy kissing and fondling Denise. The doctor and I broke it up, and by that time some of the help came and took the guy away. Needless to say, that was very upsetting to Gail and me. They had Denise on so much medication that she was like a zombie and didn't know what was going on. I hated to leave her in that hospital, but our private hospital still didn't have any rooms available. I was determined to get her out as soon as I could.

About two days after my first visit with Denise at the Ypsilanti hospital, I received a phone call from one of the workers there. She was talking in a low voice like she didn't want anyone to hear her. She asked if my wife was promiscuous, and I was shocked. I told her that my wife wasn't like that at all. She then said that they were having a hard time trying to keep the young black guy and Denise apart. Then the girl hung up the phone. The next day I received a phone call, and this time it was from Denise. I could tell that she was still drugged up, but she told me she wanted a divorce because she had met someone whom she was in love with. She said they had gone to school together. She was talking about the young black guy. I knew that they hadn't gone to school together because he was about twenty-five years old and Denise was about thirty-six at that time.

I checked in with our private hospital and a room was available. I went to the Ypsilanti hospital, checked Denise out, and got her checked into our private hospital. I swore that I would let Denise die before I would ever put her back in the Ypsilanti State Hospital. It wasn't just because of the incident with the black guy. The hospital didn't seem to have enough help, and I don't think the doctors were the best; most of them were hard to understand because they were from a foreign country.

After another four weeks in our private hospital with her own doctor taking care of her, Denise was released; it would be another two years before she had to be committed again. Denise had no memory of being in the Ypsilanti State Hospital, and for that I was thankful. I write about some of the things Denise and I went through, not to make Denise look bad because she wasn't, but to show some to the things that you live with when you are married to someone who is bipolar. Denise didn't choose to be bipolar, but that was the way she was born and she tried to make the best of it.

Denise was the best thing that ever happened to me; she made my life complete.

No Christmas Joy This Year

SOME OF THE signs of manic episodes associated with bi-polar might be doing things you later regret, such as spending lots of money. Other symptoms include finding it hard to stay focused, talking faster than usual, and appearing to be high on drugs even if you haven't taken any drugs. I had seen Denise go through all of these signs, plus others.

It was just before Christmas and Denise wanted to go shopping, but when she was high like this, I didn't want her to drive. I drove her to the mall and walked with her as she was shopping. She would get outlandish ideas about what she was shopping for. For instance, she had never worn hats, but on this day she wanted some hats and something to decorate our walls. She picked out about ten hats that she thought she needed and wanted to buy. I kept trying to talk her out of buying so many hats, but her mind was racing so fast, I don't think that she heard a word I was trying to convey to her. She also had a lot of pictures that she had intended to hang on our walls in the house. She had no theme or pattern for hanging these pictures, but she knew that she had to have them. The store was busy so we had to wait in line to check out, and I was trying to talk her out of getting so many items. She got upset with me and doubled up her fist, threatening to punch me in the nose. By this time she was speaking very loudly, and everyone started looking at us. Trying not to create a scene, I let her buy all of those hats and pictures. At times like these, I knew that she wouldn't remember them later, but I couldn't stop her from doing these things. I had to make her feel that her decisions were okay at the time. She came home and put some of her hats on and started hanging pictures; she was in her glory. It was always hard to have her committed to the hospital and put her on medication to bring her down, but she couldn't continue in that manic state of mind. She spent her first Christmas in the hospital, and I had to remove all of the pictures that she had hung and hide all of her hats. There would be no joy at Christmas this year. When she returned home, she never mentioned her hats or the pictures.

A Very Hard Decision

IT HAD BEEN three years since my dad had passed away, and my mother was still in the nursing home. My brothers, sisters, and I continued to visit her just about every Sunday. I am not sure that she even knew where she was living. One Sunday we went to visit her and there was a strange man sitting in a wheelchair in her room; he didn't or couldn't talk. We asked Mother who this man was and she said, "Well, that is George. Don't you even know your own father?" We contacted the nursing staff and asked if they would take this man back to his room, and they did. We told Mother that he wasn't our father and she couldn't continue to bring him into her room. However, Mother continued to bring that same man down to her room and try to take care of him, still thinking that he was her husband.

One day we got a phone call from the nursing home to inform us that they had to rush Mother to the hospital; she was having problems with her heart. When we all arrived at the hospital, our mother was on life support because her heart was failing. There was nothing that the doctors could do to improve her condition; her heart was just too weak to continue on its own. They told us that they could keep her alive for a while on the life support system, but we needed to make a decision about what we wanted to do. As a group we talked about the hard decision that was before us. I think one of the siblings was against taking her off life support and the rest of us agreed that we should remove the system. We told the doctor of our decision, and we all hugged Mother and said our good-byes to her. The doctor said he would wait until the next day to remove the life support, and after the support was removed, he told us that she passed away a couple hours later.

That was in 1991, and my mother was eighty years old at the time of her passing. She and my dad both passed away in March, three years apart. That was the hardest decision I ever had to make, and I hope that I am never in that position again.

Mother's funeral service was held at the Chilson Hills Baptist Church, the same place as my dad's service. Denise and I were members of this church as were my sister Irene and her family. Pastor Swink knew most of my family. In making funeral arrangements, the pastor asked if any of the kids wanted to write something about our mother that he could read during the service. I went to bed that night, but I couldn't sleep. I lay there crying and trying not to disturb Denise. I got out of bed and went to my computer room. I needed someone to talk to, so mentally I went to my dad's gravesite to let him know that mother was coming home again. This is what I wrote for the pastor to read:

Hi Dad,

No this is not Jerry; this is your baby, you remember—your big dummy, Rog. Dad, do you remember when I was twenty-one years old? You called me and said, ""Your mother is coming home; would you like to meet her?" I was very happy, very excited, but most of all very frightened. I had never seen my mother, and we didn't have any pictures of her, so I didn't know how she looked. But I had formed a mental picture of her. So on the long train ride from Lake Charles, Louisiana, to West Virginia, many questions raced through my mind. What would she look like? What would she think of me? Would she like me? Did she blame me for her illness? So many unanswered questions.

I must admit that I was a little disappointed when I first met her. She had no teeth, her hair was a mess, and her dress was torn and tattered. But nineteen years in a mental institution had not been kind to her. She didn't look like the mental picture that I had formed in my mind. But now, thirty years later, that picture has developed into a beautiful portrait of my mother. I have learned that she was a very gentle, kind, loving, and caring person. Also that she is the mother that I missed for nineteen years. Dad, do you remember the pinto beans and chicken dinners that we had every Sunday with you and Mother at your house?

Dad, I remember when you lost your eyesight and Mother took care of you. I remember how much she missed you when you passed away. So much to remember in the last thirty years.

Just as our Heavenly Father has promised, "I will go and prepare a place for you." I know that you and Walt have been doing the same. So now, Dad, I am letting you know that Mother is coming home again.

Dad, don't forget to "leave the lights on" because the rest of your kids will be coming home soon.

Rog

Denise and my mother shared a special bond. They lived in a dark world that neither one of them chose but did the best that they could to live like everyone else. When my mother passed away, Denise felt alone in that dark world; she had no one who would be able to understand what she was going through. You can read books about bipolar illness, but you will never have that hopeless feeling that Denise and my mother had to contend with for most of their lives. They knew that something was wrong with their thinking but could do nothing to change it without medication. Denise, like my mother, would become psychotic at times and wanted to kill me and our kids. She was smart enough to know that those were not her true feelings, so she would always tell her doctor and he would have her committed to the hospital to adjust her medication.

It took a while for Denise to adjust after my mother passed away, and then she had some of her best times coping with her illness. She went ten years without being in the hospital, but we would see her doctor on monthly visits.

I often think about how my life paralleled that of my dad's, but his life was much more difficult than mine. He had seven kids to raise, and I only had three. In addition, my wife was never in the hospital for more than six to eight weeks at a time, not nineteen years like my mother.

1992: Two
Major Decisions

IN 1992 DENISE was having a good year and had not been in the hospital for the last couple of years. Work was slowing down because of the poor economy (cars were not selling). General Motors was in the process of trimming their salaried employees. The company was making a special retirement offer to anyone who had over ten years of service.. I had not thought about retiring because I was only fifty-three years old, and I had almost thirty-two years of service with General Motors. In the summer of 1992, however, I was struck with psoriatic arthritis in all of my joints and had a very hard time trying to walk. I had to quit the golf league, and I was put on a high dose of steroids, but that wasn't a cure-all for arthritis. Also the steroids had a lot of bad side effects that I wasn't thrilled about. I continued to limp into work each day, with a lot of pain each step of the way to my office.

In October of that year, my superintendent called me into his office one morning and asked if I would be interested in talking to the personal director about retirement. He had noticed that I was having a hard time walking, and I told him that I would be interested in talking to the personnel director to see what my offer would be. My retirement would be based on my thirty-two years of service plus a supplement that I would get until I was sixty-two years old. I said that I needed to talk with my wife and I would let them know.

I went home and told Denise what I had been offered as a special retirement package, and right away she said I should take the offer because of the pain I was having with my arthritis. I kept thinking that fifty-three was way too young for retirement, but I also thought that if my arthritis was under control, I could do some other type of work if I felt like it. My big concern was being with Denise twenty-four hours a day with her bipolar illness. I didn't mean any disrespect to her, but it is difficult to be with someone twenty-four hours a day even if he or she is well. I took a couple of days to think about the retirement offer before I let the personal director know my decision.

After sleeping on the information, I decided to accept the retirement offer. My last day of work would be just before the Christmas holidays, and my official retirement would begin on January 1, 1993. General Motors had a big retirement dinner for all of the salaried workers who took the special offer. The skilled tradesmen also had a retirement party for me, and that one was special. I enjoyed it more because a lot of us had grown up together in our working lives. This was my first major decision of 1992.

And now for the second major decision and the rest of the story.

It was 1992 and, as I mentioned before, another engineer

and I had our own softball teams. We played a lot all summer long and had refreshments during and after the game. I was never a big drinker, and my problem was when I did drink, I would drink too much. On this day my team was getting our butts kicked, and that may have been the reason that I drank more than I should have. After the game was over and we lost twelve to six, I had a couple more beers. Then I needed to pee, but we didn't have any restrooms available so I went down to the river. As I was standing on the edge of the riverbank peeing, I fell in the river. It wasn't one of those "Hallelujah, I see the light" moments, but it was an "I don't need this shit" moment, and I haven't had a drink of alcohol since that date in 1992. Again, I never had a problem with uncontrolled drinking, but when I did drink, I would overdo it, get sick, and end up hugging the commode and throwing up. Denise would help by flushing the commode. So I made up my mind that day that I could live without falling into the river and without hugging the commode. Some men want to fight when they drink, but when I drank, I became the world's greatest lover. Move over, Rudolph Valentino, Rog has had a few beers. Then I realized it was all in my head. Those were the two major decisions that I made in 1992, and I haven't regretted making either one of them.

Life after Retirement

ONE DAY I was down in my basement doing something, and my daughter Gail was taking a shower in the big bathroom. I noticed that water was leaking into the basement as she showered. I had never used that bathroom so I wasn't aware that we had a leaking problem. I started checking out the problem and could tell that this had been an issue for a long time. It looked like I needed to replace the bathroom floor, so I began to remove everything in the bathroom. I had to remove the tub and the first row of tile above the tub, as well as the commode, the two sinks, and the cabinets. Then I had to remove the floor in the bathroom and install new plywood flooring. After the floor had been replaced, everything was put back into the bathroom, and I then installed new ceramic tile on the floor. I also installed ceramic title in the other bathroom and the laundry room, and I purchased and installed new cabinets for both bathrooms. This project kept me busy for two months, and just as I had completed the project, I received a phone call from General Motors. They wanted to know if I would be interested in working as a skilled trades supervisor for the summer. It would only be for three months to cover for vacations, and I would be paid thirty-one dollars an hour plus my full retirement. I told them that I would do it.

About that same time I was put on Enbrel injections for my arthritis, and that was making a big difference in how I was feeling. I was able to start playing golf again, but the Enbrel didn't improve my golf score. I was just happy to be playing golf again. Those three months at GM turned into eight years but as a contract employee. During those eight years, Denise was doing well at controlling her illness with medication and monthly visits with her psychiatrist. We took long vacations in the summertime and traveled in our motor home. We had also started square dancing, along with my two sisters and two of my brothers and their spouses. We traveled a lot to attend square dances in many states. Denise and I both enjoyed the traveling and the dancing. Retirement was good.

After working eight more years for GM after my retirement, my brother Dennis and his wife, Beverly, were the ones who got us involved in square dancing. Several of our friends with whom we square-danced spent their winters in Texas because square dancing was very popular there and some of the best callers owned clubs down there. Dennis and Beverly were the first in our family to spend their winter in Texas, and they told Denise and I how great it was—we could play golf all winter. So Denise and I decided we would go to Texas in the winter to see how we liked it—and we did like the warm weather, the friendly people, and golfing all winter. So I notified GM that I would be leaving for Texas and would not be able to work for the company anymore, but they said they would call me in April when I got home to see if I was interested in working again.

Our son Tony had started his family, and he and Margaret had two boys, our first grandkids. Our oldest daughter, Pamela, and her husband, Tod, would have two boys and our only granddaughter. Denise was enjoying the grandkids so much because she was feeling so much better. She always felt bad because she couldn't be the kind of mother she wanted to be to her own kids. When they were small, Denise spent most of her time in the hospital. So it was good to watch her with our grandkids and to see how much she loved them. You would think that Denise was born in the South because she called everyone "honey." She had so much love in her heart, especially for her grandkids. It was good to see Denise be the kind of mother that she always wanted to be through her grandkids. It would bring tears to my eyes as I watched her shower our grandkids with so much love, something that the bipolar illness robbed her of when our kids were small. She loved our kids but couldn't express that feeling the way she could now with our grandkids. She did a very good job of expressing her love for our kids when they were older; today each one of our kids knows how much she loved them.

In January 2001, Denise and I loaded up our motor home and headed to Texas for the winter. We would be staying in the same park as my brother Dennis and his wife, Beverly. This would be their third year of wintering in Texas. We also knew other couples from our square dance club back in Michigan who were staying in the same park. We had snow when we left Michigan, but when we arrived in McAllen, Texas, they were cutting the green grass along the highway, and there were palm trees along the highways and fields of oranges and grapefruits everywhere. I had only been in Texas once, back in 1957, when

I was in basic training at Lackland Air Force Base. Back then we didn't get to leave the base, so I didn't know that much about Texas. In the last sixteen years I have learned a lot about the state and have enjoyed my time there. Denise and I visited a lot of interesting places. There were so many places to eat and so many things to do, we were busy all winter long learning about the area. There also were several entertainers from Branson, Missouri, who came to Texas in the winter because things were slow back in Branson. Denise and I made many new friends in the park, and they are still friends today. We enjoyed our first winter in Texas, so we made reservations for the next winter. The first winter we were in Texas Trails RV Park, there were 1,472 people in the park.

When we got back to Michigan, I wanted something to do but wasn't sure I wanted to go back to GM. We had a country club close to our house, and there was a sign that said it needed people to cut the grass on the golf course. I went over to talk with them and was offered a job; I was paid eight dollars per hour for cutting the grass. I had been working there about two weeks when I received a call from GM. The company offered me a job at thirty-one dollars per hour, but I told them that forty years was enough. I enjoyed working outside and being on the golf course, plus we could play golf every Monday for free. I was only working four days a week, and it gave me something to do and a chance to get out of the house.

Texas, Our Second Home

AFTER OUR FIRST year of living in Texas through the winters, we would spend the next thirteen winters there. We had met so many nice people, and we were very busy all winter long. Each year when April appeared on the calendar, it was kind of sad because it was time to head back to Michigan and leave all of our new friends; we wouldn't see them again until late December. Denise kept busy all winter making hats for cancer patients who had lost their hair and also for newborn babies to keep their heads warm. She took them to different hospitals so they could pass them out to the people who needed or wanted one. She remained busy when we were back in Michigan; she wanted to help the cancer patients in any way that she could. Every week we had a guy who came to our park and sold vegetables and fruits from his truck. Denise always bought a fifteen-pound bag of oranges, and we used our juicer to make 120 ounces of fresh orange juice. Denise gave it all to some of the older people in our park; it was in her heart to try to help other people. She would also make two packs of Toll House chocolate chip cookies and pass them out to our friends. She became known as the Cookie Lady. Again, she just wanted to please people; it made her feel good that she could help someone.

During the second year we were in Texas, we met a very nice couple from Maine. We went swimming with them every day and went out to eat about twice a week. One day, in the swimming pool, they told me that they had started doing wood carving and that I should go with them to learn how to do it. I knew nothing about carving, and I didn't have any carving tools. The couple said that they had never done any carving and had no tools, but the man in charge of the wood-carvers had tools and would help me get started. So that was the beginning of my love affair with wood carving, and after fourteen years I still love it. I soon found out that wood carving is only about 10 percent and the other 90 percent is BS, and I am good at that 90 percent.

I was getting very involved with my newfound passion. I had spent a lot of money on wood-carving tools and different types of carving classes. A wood-carving project wasn't just carving; it included wood burning and painting. Wood carving was very popular in our park; at one time we had seventy-two people in our Texas Trails Wood Carving Club, and some of us belonged to another club, the Rio Grand Wood-Carvers. We had about 310 people in that club. Each year the Rio Grand Wood-Carvers put on a show, and more than two thousand people attended. Carvers could enter their projects into the show to be judged, and there were many different types of carving entries on display. Over the years I entered some of my projects, and I was able (and lucky) to win one blue ribbon for first place, two red ribbons for second place, and one white ribbon for a third-place finish.

Because of the hobbies that Denise and I had, our motor home was getting too small with all of our projects in it. We decided that we needed a bigger place, so we bought a 12-by-33-foot park model with a 10-by-22-foot Texas room added onto it. It was so nice having all of that extra room, plus a washer and dryer. We were in hog heaven. We enjoyed that place for the next five years, and then we sold it because of health problems. The next year we rented a place to stay at Texas Trails RV Resort; that would be Denise's last year in Texas for the winter.

We got back to Michigan in April 2012, and Denise was having some problems with her bladder. We made an appointment with a doctor who wanted to do a CAT scan of her bladder. Nothing showed up on her bladder, but he noticed a mass buildup on her pancreas. He told us that it might be nothing, but we should have it checked out by an oncologist. We talked to several doctors, and it was recommended that Denise have a biopsy. Two different doctors looked at the CAT scan of her pancreas, and both said it didn't look like cancer, but they made an appointment for her biopsy to be sure.

Denise and Gail outside our winter home in Mcallen, Texas.

Happy Thanksgiving

IT WAS NOVEMBER and we had an appointment for Denise to have the biopsy on her pancreas. We were not too concerned because two different doctors had said they didn't think it was cancer. They said they would call us when the lab work was completed and give us the results. It was about five days after Denise had the biopsy, at about 5:00 p.m. on November 21, 2012, and the next day was Thanksgiving. The phone rang and I answered it. The man on the other end said that he was Dr. Zeglis and he would like to have Denise on the phone also. I called into another room and had Denise pick up the phone. Then Dr. Zeglis informed us that it was cancer on her pancreas. I just about fell on the floor. After we hung up the phone, I ran to Denise, hugged her, and starting crying, and then she started crying. I became so upset with God. I yelled out to him, asking him why he would do this to her. Hadn't she suffered enough the last forty-six years with bipolar disorder? By this time Denise had quit crying and came over to me and tried to calm me down. She put her arms around me and told me that God was using her to help other people. I wanted to know why God hadn't asked me if it was okay to use Denise. Hadn't forty-six years been enough to help other people? I also wanted to know why the doctors hadn't waited until the day after Thanksgiving to tell us the bad news; we could have enjoyed our Thanksgiving more.

I made the phone calls to our kids, and it was one of the hardest things I have ever had to do. It was also the hardest Thanksgiving we ever had as a family. I didn't feel as though we had anything to be thankful for. In fact there were many things to be thankful for, but I couldn't see them at the time. I was still angry with God, and I didn't say the prayer before we ate our dinner. I was probably wrong for feeling that way, but I had so much pain in my heart. I knew there was no cure for pancreatic cancer; it was just a matter of time and how much more she would have to suffer. After the holidays, we made appointments to see a doctor and find out what our options were if she chose surgery.

My Purpose in Life

LONG BEFORE RICK Warren wrote his book *The Purpose Driven Life*, I always believed that God had a purpose planned for me. I look back on so many things that had to be in place for Denise and me to be in the same place and at the right time. When I was discharged from the Air Force six months early, if I had gone to live with my brother Walt, I may have never met Denise. Walt lived about six miles from where Irene lived. If I had been discharged six months later, we may have never met. But I chose to live with my sister Irene and her family, and she lived just down the street from Denise and her family. Denise was born in Montreal, Quebec, Canada, and I was born in Excelsior, West Virginia. How were we going to meet if God didn't have a plan for us? God's plan started long before Denise and I met. I was born on the side of a mountain, but God placed a bigger mountain in my life. I was going to be raised without the love of my mother and all of the things that a mother teaches her children, but I was raised by my dad, who was very strong in his faith in God and he led by example. I learned so much from watching him, and the way he lived his life would help me later on in my own life. It seemed as though God was preparing me for what was to come when he placed another big mountain in my life: Denise's diagnosis of bipolar disorder.

On June 23, 1961, the day that Denise and I met, there were other things that could have changed my life, but God was still in control. I originally had asked Denise's girlfriend Diane to go out with me, but she said no. I found out later that the reason she said no was because she'd had an abortion about two months earlier; she didn't want anything to do with guys at that point in her life. What would have happened if Diane had agreed to go out with me? Would Denise and I ever have gone out on a date? I don't know the answer to that, but I still think it was part of God's plan. He knew that Denise would need help in her life later on, so his plan was to bring us together because I had learned so much from watching my dad and how he was able to keep all seven of his kids together as a family. He did it without the help of his wife, who was in a mental hospital for nineteen years. My dad was able to do this because each one of us kids had chores to do and was responsible for certain things that would keep the house operating as it should.

God's plan was coming together as Denise and I started dating. One year later on June 23, 1962, we got married and started our family. We had been married about seven years when God placed the huge mountain (Denise's diagnosis) in front of me, and we had three kids when this happened. I was so thankful that my parents were able to live with me when Denise was first committed to Mercywood Psychiatric Hospital in Ann Arbor, Michigan, in 1969. After forty-six years—most of them rough on Denise—I felt like we were able to climb this huge mountain that God had placed before us. Most of it was accomplished with the help of family and friends and a strong faith in God. I hope that I never missed the opportunity to say thank-you to my family for all of their support as we were climbing that mountain.

Just as it seemed like Denise and I had reached the top of that bipolar mountain, enjoying life and spending our winters in Texas, God placed a much larger mountain in front of us. Denise had been diagnosed with pancreatic cancer. This mountain was too large, and we would not be able to climb and/or conquer it like we had done on the other mountains. This was God's plan, and I couldn't do anything to change it. It didn't help that I got so angry with God, but I am only human and I couldn't change God's plan. As we got older, when I said my prayer before going to sleep, I would ask God to take Denise first. It sounds like I was being selfish, but I didn't want my kids to have to take care of their mother; it was a very hard job, and I had been prepared to take care of her. I wasn't always right, but I did the best that I could with the gift that God had planned for me, Denise.

The Long Journey

AFTER RECEIVING THE bad news that Denise had pancreatic cancer, we had the worst Thanksgiving dinner ever because no one wanted to eat. We made an appointment to see a surgeon and find out what our options were to try to overcome this cancer. He gave us two options. If we did nothing, she might have six months to live, and if we chose to have surgery to remove part of her pancreas, she could have up to twenty-four months. Both of our girls were with us, and I did not voice my feelings one way or the other. I wanted that decision to be made by Denise and our girls. The doctor told us that it was a major surgery, and the recovery could be long and hard. After talking for sometime, Denise decided that she wanted to have the surgery. Our doctor set up a date for her surgery, and it was to be done on December 17, 2012. All of my family, our three kids, my brothers, my sister, and her daughter; Judy, who was Denise's best friend; and the pastor of our church sat with me. After a long 7½ hours of surgery, the doctor came to talk with us. He said that he had removed about 70 percent of her pancreas, as well as her gallbladder and spleen, but the surgery went well. She would need a long time in rehab to recover from the surgery. When she had recovered from the surgery, she would need radiation and chemo treatments.

While she was in the hospital, her surgeon took her off the lithium that she had been on for forty-two years. He said she had been on it so long that it was causing problems with her kidneys and could cause them to quit working. As a family, we didn't think Denise would be able to function without the lithium, but her psychiatrist put her on another medication to replace it. We couldn't believe how much better Denise sounded, and she was more aware of things around her. Her thinking and thought process were much clearer. She was released from the hospital and sent to a rehab center, but she had to be sent back to the hospital the next day because of complications. After three days back in the hospital, she was transported to rehab again.

After the long surgery that Denise went through, she would spend almost three months in the rehab center. I went to sit with her every day. She wanted me to bring her some yarn and her knitting needles from home so she could continue making hats for cancer patients who had lost their hair. She had been doing this for several years and would drop them off at different hospital to give to their patients. That was Denise; even though she was suffering from cancer, she was always thinking of people she thought were worse off than she was.

It took Denise a long time to build up her strength to the point where she was able to walk. Before she could walk, Denise spent a lot of her time just lying in bed, and because of that she developed a large bedsore on her tailbone. The doctors at the rehab center treated this bedsore for a long time, but it kept getting larger. They called in a doctor who was a certified wound specialist, and after he started treating her, she began to get better. He was using Medihoney, a special type of honey indigenous to New Zealand. She was strong enough to be released from the rehab center, but her bedsore was far from being healed. The specialist showed me how to clean out the wound each day and then pack it with the Medihoney; it still took a long time to heal because of its size. I was amazed at how it healed up and closed.

After her three-month stay in the rehab center, Denise started losing weight, but she maintained such a positive attitude throughout all of her time after the cancer surgery. She started the oncology radiation treatments, and after they were completed, she started the chemo treatments. They installed a port in her chest to make it easier for the infusion of the chemo treatments. I have so many pictures of her taken with my iPad as she endured her treatments. In every one of the pictures, she was smiling and knitting a hat for some other cancer patient. She always told me that God was using her to help other people—and that she did.

After Surgery, the Good Times

AFTER DENISE WAS taken off of the lithium medication she had been on for about forty-two years, she started to feel much better, and she became a person that our kids had never seen. She was much more alert and spoke with a lot more confidence. She was doing so well. Denise and I hadn't been able to travel for two years because of her cancer. We were invited to the wedding of my great-nephew Russell Harkai. He was born and raised in Michigan, but his family moved to Franklin, Tennessee, when he was a teenager. While he still lived in Michigan, his dad and his brother would spend a week up in northern Michigan during bow hunting season with the rest of the Evans clan. When Russel, his brother Ryan, and their cousins Jason and Nick were little, I taught them how to eat acorns. We were sitting around the campfire one night and I had some acorns that I had picked up. I used my hunting knife to open them, and then I pretended to eat the acorns. All four of them wanted to know what I was doing, and I told them I was eating acorns. They asked me if they tasted good. "Sure, they taste good," I told them. So all four of them wanted to try some of the acorns. I cut the shell off several acorns and gave each one a couple to eat. They put them in their mouth and starting chewing. It wasn't long before each one of the boys started spitting their acorns out of their mouth. If you have never eaten acorns, don't because they are very bitter. I could have told the four boys how they tasted, but showing them how they tasted would be with them for the rest of their lives.

Russel, Ryan, Jason, and Nick were with us every year during bow hunting season, plus they lived close to Denise and me. So when we got the invitation to Russel's wedding, we wanted to attend. Denise was feeling good, so we loaded up our car and drove just a few miles each day. It took us two days to make the five-hundred-mile trip, but I wanted to make sure that Denise would be okay. Most of my brothers and sisters would be there with their kids and grandkids. Many of them hadn't seen Denise since her surgery.

The wedding was held in a Tennessee state park just west of Nashville. They were married in a beautiful chapel, and the dinner and reception were held in the resort where we all stayed. It was a beautiful setting for a wedding, and I am so glad that Denise and I got to attend. It would be the last time that many members of my family would see Denise. After the dinner, there was the usual music you have at every wedding, such as the chicken dance. I went outside and was talking to some of the guys, and Denise was sitting with my two sisters inside. Someone came running to me and said, "Roger, get inside; they are playing your song." I went inside to the dance floor and saw a few couples dancing to John Denver's song "Country Roads." Denise was already on the dance floor waiting for me, and when Denise and I started dancing, everyone else left the dance floor. I have never seen so many camera flashes and iPads recording our last dance. When I was holding Denise in my arms and kissing her at every opportunity I could get, I felt just like the song says: "Almost Heaven, West Virginia."

To think that this beautiful French girl from Montreal would meet a country boy from West Virginia and become his wife for fifty-two years, three months, and seventeen days, God was good to me. I have always loved that John Denver song, but now when I hear it, it fills my heart and makes me think about Denise and our last dance. I was so happy that we could attend Russel's wedding. His brother Ryan got married about five months later in Florida, but we couldn't attend the wedding because Denise was getting weaker.

When Denise was faced with the decision of doing nothing or having surgery, I am glad that she chose to have the surgery because we had some good quality time after her stay at the rehab center. I don't know what my decision would be if I was faced with the same situation, and I may never know.

Her Last Birthday

IT HAD BEEN twenty-one months since Denise had her cancer surgery, and the doctor had told her that she might live twenty-four months after the surgery. During the last twenty-one months, we had some quality time with Denise. The rehab had been rough, but since rehab she had been such a joy to be with, always smiling and wanting to help other people. She was also starting to lose more weight and have less energy. We had a nurse coming to our house every week to check on her. This nurse was such a great lady, and we developed a good friendship with her. Denise looked forward to seeing her each week, and we would talk about her health and any fears that she may have about what to expect in the coming months. One day we were sitting at the kitchen table with the nurse, and Denise started crying. I asked what was wrong, and she looked at me with tears in her eyes and said, "I have failed you again; I let you down." The only words I could think of at the time were "No, no, no, don't ever think that again. God has a plan for us." I had so much pain in my heart when she said that she had failed me; never did I feel as though she had failed me. She did the best that she could do with her bipolar illness.

It was August 18, 2014, and Denise turned seventy-one years old. Our two girls, Pam and Gail; our grandson Kyle; and I took Denise to one of her favorite restaurants, Red Lobster, in Ann Arbor for her birthday, and Gail had a big chocolate chip cookie, the size of a large pizza, to celebrate the occasion. After a very good dinner, we cut into the chocolate chip cookie. The thing that I remember the most about her last birthday is how beautiful she looked. She had been through a lot during the last two years, but there was that ever-present smile of hers and she was so pretty. I wish the whole world could have seen her that day and try to understand how someone who had been through so much in her lifetime still could smile, knowing what must be in God's plan for her. My plan is to join her again so I can see that beautiful smile on her face.

Denise's 71ˢᵗ birthday with her two daughters, Pam and Gail.

Nothing We Can Do

DENISE WASN'T FEELING good one morning when she got out of bed, so I told her to get ready; I was going to take her to see our doctor. When our doctor came in to see Denise, the first words out of his mouth were "You don't look good; you need to be in the hospital." Denise just smiled at him and said that she was going to be okay and didn't want to go to the hospital. So we went back home. The pain in her stomach was getting worse, though, so I told her that I was taking her to the hospital. She was admitted, and after the nurse got all of her medical history, they started running different tests and taking X-rays and an MRI to try to find the root cause of her stomach pain. On the second day, they found out that there was a blockage in her intestines. They stuck a tube into her nose and down to her stomach to try to remove everything in her stomach. They left the tube in for two days, but the blockage wasn't getting any better. They didn't know what was causing the blockage. They said it could be because of scar tissue from the surgery or it could be the cancer was active again. There was a chance that they could operate and clear up the blockage, but by this time they didn't think Denise was strong enough to survive another surgery.

I was there with Denise every day, and all of our kids would come after work. One evening when we were all there, the doctor in charge got us together in another room and told us that there was "nothing we can do"—very chilling words that none of us wanted to hear. Denise had been in the hospital for six days and had not eaten anything, nor was she able to drink any water. One of the doctors told us that we should think about putting her in hospice and they offered to help us set it up. The hospital had its own hospice unit, but we went with the Ann Arbor Hospice because we knew other people who'd had their family members there and were happy with the care their family member had received. We called the Ann Arbor Hospice to arrange for a medical bed to be set up in our house.

The Ann Arbor Hospice delivered a medical bed, and I had them set it up in front of the fireplace. We would be able to raise the bed so Denise could see the deer in our yard just off the end of our deck. The hospital released her, and she was transported to our home and put into the medical bed, where she would spend her last nine days. Still unable to eat or drink, she wasn't able to talk very much to any of us. Ann Arbor Hospice came and checked on her and gave us the medication that we would be giving her. They also told us that their job wasn't to try to heal her but to make her remaining days more comfortable. They gave us morphine to make sure that she wouldn't suffer from any pain. For some reason Denise always kept her eyes on me when I was in the room. If I got up and moved, her eyes followed me. We pulled one of the La-Z-Boy recliners up next to her bed, and one of us would sleep next to her and hold her hand as we also tried to get some sleep. She was still unable to eat or drink, and one day, as I was starting to take a bite of pizza, she surprised us and said, "No, Roger." Each time I took a bite she repeated the same words. I don't know why she was saying that; it was almost as if she was thinking that I shouldn't eat or drink because she wanted me to go on this journey with her as she was nearing the "valley of the shadow of death." For fifty-two years I always held her hand anytime we went anywhere, and I really felt as though she wanted me to go with her. I wish I could have.

It was Sunday morning, October12, 2014, and I had gotten up at about five thirty. Gail was sleeping in the recliner next to her mother. I went over to check on Denise and she was barely breathing, so I made myself a cup of coffee and went into the living room. Just a few minutes later Gail came into the living room and told me it was over; Mom was not breathing. After crying and hugging each other, Gail called Tony and Pam to let them know that their mother was in heaven now. We also had to call Ann Arbor Hospice so they could send someone to pronounce her dead.

The Golden Years

I WANT TO talk about what Denise and I referred to as the golden years of our life. When we were young and raising our three kids, Denise had most of her problems caused by her bipolar illness. Now that we were older and were enjoying our five grandkids, this was more like what we would call the golden years. We went to football games, soccer games, and gymnastics competitions that our grandkids were participating in. Aaron and Derek were the two oldest grandkids, and they were both into football. They would also go into the military, with Aaron serving one year in Iraq and one year in Afghanistan. Josh, Kyle, and Carlie were into soccer, and Carlie also was in gymnastics. Denise and I went to see Carlie compete in gymnastics, but we were always afraid that she was going to get hurt.

We loved all five of our grandkids, but I must admit that Carlie held a special place in our hearts. She was the youngest and the only girl. Denise and I took care of her more than the others because our daughter Pamela had gone back to work. When Carlie was about two years old, she was still in diapers though she should have been potty-trained. One day, as we were babysitting, I noticed that Carlie was standing in the corner and straining to poop. She looked up and saw me watching her and said, "Don't look, Grandpa." If she was smart enough to say that, she should have been potty-trained.

When she was three years old, we were babysitting and had been playing on the floor and doing different things. At that point in my life, I was starting to be forgetful. For instance, later that day while I was taking my shower and singing some doo-wop songs as I always did when showering, I looked down and couldn't believe what I saw. Lying on the floor of the shower were eight or ten large gold nuggets. I couldn't believe my eyes, but there they were. So I got out of the shower and started drying off. Then I noticed that those gold nuggets were now lying on the bathroom floor. I wiped my eyes and put on my glasses so I could get a better look at those gold nuggets. My gosh! Those were not nuggets; those were my toes, but why were they painted gold? At that moment I remembered that my three-year-old granddaughter had painted them. I may have lost a fortune, but I gained so much love from my granddaughter for letting her paint my toes. She was so proud of the paint job too. Now I had to find the nail polish remover; I sure would hate to have an accident and end up in the hospital with gold toes. After I had finished my shower, I also realized that I needed to lose some weight. You know that you are overweight when you take a shower, dry off, and bend over to put on your socks and about a half cup of water falls out of your bellybutton. I think that a half cup is equal to about twenty-five pounds of needed weight loss.

When Carlie was about five years old, she had come home

with Denise and me to spend the weekend with us. After she had been with us for two days, her dad was coming to pick her up. Carlie and I were sitting on the front porch, waiting for her dad, and she said to me, "Grandpa, I have been here for two days, but it seems like it has been a week." I told her that I knew it was hard for young kids to sit with old people for such a long time. It's hard to believe that Josh and Kyle are in college now and Carlie is visiting colleges to see where she wants to go next year. All of our grandkids made this the golden years for Denise and me. She loved them all so very much. Denise would make cookies and ship them to Aaron and Derek and was always praying for their safe return.

I was so proud of all of our grandkids at Denise's memorial service. Derek was the main speaker for all of the grandkids, and they were all at the front of the church as he spoke. When he finished, there wasn't a dry eye in the church, and each one of our grandkids with their wives came over to me, hugged me, and told me they loved me. In fact there isn't a dry eye at this computer now as I type. Thank God for the golden years that I got to spend with Denise and our grandkids.

*Our grandkids: Kyle, Josh, Grandpa Rog, Grandma Denise,
Aaron, Carlie, Brittany (Aaron's wife), and Derek.*

Cremation

DENISE PASSED AWAY on October 12, 2014, and her wish was to be cremated so there would be no viewing. When the funeral director came to our house to pick up her body, he placed some flowers near her body and let each one of us say our good-byes to Denise. Each one of us spent some time with her, and as we were crying and saying good-bye, we each kissed her for the final time. After she was cremated, Denise's ashes were placed in the Cross Columbarium at the Chilson Hill Church Memorial Garden; this was the same place that her mother and dad's ashes had been placed. We had a beautiful memorial service about three weeks after her passing. The church had to bring out more chairs to accommodate the people who had come to pay their last respects. It was very heartwarming to see how much Denise had meant to so many people.

Denise would ask me what I wanted done with my body after I died, and I would always tell her that it didn't matter to me what she did with my body. She told me that she wanted me cremated and placed in the niche next to her. So that was our plan. I used to kid her and say, "Yes, I want to be cremated because that will be my last chance for a hot, smoking body." She would get upset with me because she didn't think that I should be kidding about cremation.

It has been almost two years since Denise passed away, and they have been the worst two years of my life. There is not a day that goes by that I don't think about her and want to see that beautiful smile of hers and just hold her hand like I did for fifty-two years, three months, and seventeen days. Love you, Denise.

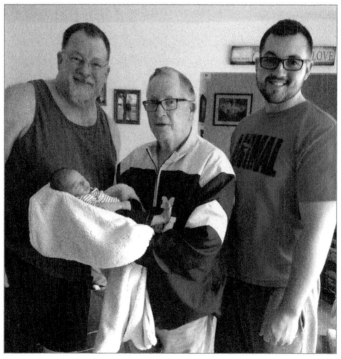

This is the future of the Evans' clan. Four generations: Tony Louis, Roger Louis, Derek Lewis, and Wesley Lewis Evans.

Acknowledgments

I HAVE HAD people in my life who knew about my childhood and my married life, and they told me that I should write
a book about my life. I am not a professional writer as you
know by now, but I did want people to know about my dad
and my wife, Denise, the two most influential people in my
life, and what they meant to me. George Wesley Evans, my
father, taught me so much about life, not by reading books to
me but by being an example of how to live my life. Through
his strong faith in God, he was able to raise seven kids and keep
us all together after my mother was committed to a mental
hospital in West Virginia. She would spend the next nineteen
years in that hospital. She was committed in 1941 when I was
just two years old, and I didn't meet her until I was twenty-one
years old. I also wanted to show how my life paralleled the life
of my dad.

Denise Legault was a French Canadian born in Montreal,
Quebec, Canada, who came to the United States in 1956 at the
age of twelve. At that time no one in her family could speak
English. She and I met in 1961 after I had gotten out of the

Air Force and moved to Ypsilanti, Michigan. We started dating and were married one year later in 1962. After having three kids, Denise was diagnosed as being bipolar and was hospitalized thirty-four times in our fifty-two years of marriage. My parents were a big help when Denise was in the hospital and I had to work. It was during this time that I recalled how my dad was able to raise his seven kids, and I was going to try to live by his example.

I truly believe that God had a purpose for me, and it was to bring Denise and me together so I could use what I had learned from watching my dad as I took care of Denise and our three kids. So many things had to happen for this hillbilly kid from the mountains of West Virginia to meet and marry this beautiful French girl from Montreal. Most people will say that it was just fate, but I truly believe that I had a purpose-driven life.

My dad and Denise were the two most influential people in my life, but I owe so much to so many people, starting back in Excelsior, West Virginia, where I was born, with the Blankenship family. They were the greatest neighbors anyone could ask for. There were Clarence, Ernest, Wayne, Shelby, and Anita when I was growing up there, but three more kids were born after we moved to Atwell, West Virginia. These were the most formative years of my life, and the Blankenship family was a big part of them. My siblings Walter, Robert, Jerry, Betty, Irene, and Dennis were the ones who raised me when our dad was at work, and I owe each one of them so much. Without the love and support of our three kids—Tony, Pamela, and Gail—I don't know if I could have made it through these last two years. Sometimes I forget that my three kids have been suffering just as much as I have since their mother passed away, but my hope is that one day we will all join together as a family in heaven.

This ends my story, and I hope that you have enjoyed reading it.

TO:

Hope that you will
enjoy Reading my
life story.

Your Friend

Roger L Evans

CPSIA information can be obtained
at www.ICGtesting.com
Printed in the USA
FSOW04n2224280117
30108FS